PILGRIM PREACHER
PALESTINE, PILGRIMAGE AND PREACHING

Duncan Macpherson

with a foreword by
Naim Ateek

An enquiry into the impact of the Holy Land
upon the preaching of the Gospel with an argument for the wider relevance
of the Holy Land in all its aspects.

MELISENDE
LONDON

Pilgrim Preacher
Palestine, Pilgrimage and Preaching
by Duncan Macpherson

First published 2004 by
Melisende
39 Chelmsford Road
London E18 2PW
Tel. +44 (0)20 8498 9768
Fax +44 (0)20 8504 2558
E mail: melisende@btinternet.com
www.melisende.com
ISBN 1 901764 39 7

Editor: Leonard Harrow
Printed at the Cromwell Press, Trowbridge, England

CONTENTS

Bible versions

Unless otherwise stated texts quoted in this book are from the *Jerusalem Bible* version of the Scriptures published by Darton, Longman and Todd, London, 1966, 1967 and 1969.

Where other versions are used they are indicated as follows:
—*The Grail Psalter*, Collins (Fontana Books), London, 1966: [G]
—*The New Jerusalem Bible*, Darton, Longman and Todd , London, 1984: [NJB]
—*Revised Standard Version*, British and Foreign Bible Society,
      London 1971: [RSV]

FOREWORD

In *Pilgrim Preacher,* Duncan Macpherson sees concern for the Holy Land as a matter of importance not only for leaders of pilgrim groups, but as having a wider relevance for all involved in the proclamation of the Christian message. *Pilgrim Preacher* is about preaching, but it also considers a range of issues including the nature of Christian pilgrimage, Christian ecumenism, inter-faith relationships, and the history and resolution of the Israeli-Palestinian conflict. This should add to Christian understanding of peace and justice issues in the Holy Land and the concerns that these should arouse in the wider human community. The threat to the survival of the indigenous churches emerges as one particularly important issue among the others.

As a Christian Palestinian who has spent much of his life trying to combine the quest for justice in the Holy Land with a parallel quest for peace and reconciliation, I can only welcome *Pilgrim Preacher* as a powerful contribution towards the same cause. Although all preachers of the Gospel share a common interest in the Holy Land, their interest is too often limited to the area of biblical history. Usually their interest stops there. Where it goes further it often relates to just one chapter of history, sometimes in a one-sided manner that regards the setting up of the state of Israel in 1948 and the Israeli conquest of Jerusalem in 1967 as the fulfilment of biblical prophecy. At the same time most preachers completely ignore the historic injustice experienced by the Palestinian people.

The virtue of *Pilgrim Preacher* is that it sets out to demonstrate the relevance of the Holy Land in all its aspects for preaching. These aspects include the geographical, the cultural, the historical and the contemporary. The book also engages with the hopes and aspirations of two peoples (Palestinians and Israelis) and three faiths (Christians, Jews and Muslims). However, this breadth of scope does not mean any absence of passion for justice or commitment to the oppressed. Duncan writes from the standpoint of Liberation Theology, the perspective of our own *Sabeel* centre here in the Holy Land—a perspective taken up by our friends all over the world. What makes *Pilgrim Preacher* such a valuable contribution is that it brings together this perspective with the latest and the best in the practice and modern theory of preaching.

Canon Naim Ateek
Epiphany 2004, Sabeel, *Jerusalem*

ACKNOWLEDGEMENTS

This book is adapted from the text of a thesis submitted in partial fulfilment of the requirement for a Doctor of Ministry degree at the Aquinas Institute at St Louis, Missouri. I would first like to express my very great appreciation and thanks to the Reverend Professor Dr Gregory Heille, OP, of Aquinas, and to the Very Reverend Dr Michael Prior, CM, Senior Fellow of the Holy Land Research Project at St Mary's College, Strawberry Hill, for their advice and encouragement, both in the writing of the thesis and in the translation of the thesis into a publishable form.

For assistance in the area of modern Middle Eastern history I would like to register special thanks to Dr Nur Masalha, Director of the Holy Land Research Project. Thanks are also due to Chris Doyle, Director of the Council for the Advancement of Arab British Understanding, and to Gillian Watt and Matthew Jackson, research officers at the Council for the Advancement of Arab British Understanding.

For providing empirical research data on the experience of preachers who had visited the Holy Land I must thank the respondents on Fishers Net, members of the Upper Thames Deanery in the Archdiocese of Westminster, additional priest respondents, Father Terry Tastard and Dr Robin Gibbons, and the committee of Friends of *Sabeel*, UK. I also owe a special word of thanks to Canon Lucy Winkett of St Paul's Cathedral for her kindness in allowing me an interview.

I would also like to thank all those who evaluated or helped me to find others to evaluate my preaching. These include Father Jim McCormack, the parish priest of our Lady of Light, Clacton on Sea, and his parishioners, Adrian and Celia Cassidy and other friends who comprise the congregation of Twickenham United Reformed Church, and colleagues and friends who evaluated my homily at Venice, Florida. Very special thanks are also due to my friend and fellow student, James Hayes, who arranged my visit to Iowa State University and to the members of his 'partners in preaching team.'

Finally, I would also like to express my debt to Alan Wall and Leonard Harrow for help in editing the text of the thesis, and to Leonard Harrow and Alan Ball for help in preparing the text for publication. I would also wish to thank my wife Ann for her patient advice and moral support.

Duncan Macpherson
London 2004

INTRODUCTION

And they returned to Jerusalem with great joy and were continually in the temple blessing God (Luke 24: 52-3)[RSV].

The purpose of this study is to enquire into the relevance of the Holy Land for homiletics, and it will argue for the wider relevance of the Holy Land in all its aspects (geographical and cultural, historical and contemporary) for the preaching of the Christian message. It is hoped that such a project will contribute to the development of good preaching through its exploration of questions relating to exegesis and hermeneutics, as well as to homiletic skills.

It will address the nature of Christian pilgrimage as well as a number of other issues and problems including Christian ecumenism, inter-faith relationships (between Jews and Christians, Muslims and Christians, Muslims and Jews), and then the complexities of the Israeli-Palestinian conflict. This last should lead to a more profound understanding of peace and justice issues in the Holy Land and their relevance to the wider global perspective. The threat to the survival of the indigenous churches will stand out as a matter of particular concern to those in the Christian diaspora.

This perspective is central to the preaching of those involved in leading pilgrimage groups in the Holy Land, but it will be argued that the Holy Land has a wider relevance for all those involved in communicating the Christian message. The discussion that follows examines the impact of the Holy Land upon the preaching of the Gospel. It also sets out to explore the wider relevance of 'Holy Land Studies' for all who are involved in communicating the Christian message, providing a critical examination of the problems, challenges and opportunities for preaching within a Holy Land perspective. These include the nature of the relationship between symbol and event and the relevance of the geography and archaeology of the Holy Land for exploring this relationship. They also involve the relationship between a contextual theology of the Holy Land and the practicalities of translating that essential commitment to contextual theology through the application of appropriate and effective preaching strategies.[1] The principles

---

[1] 'To insist upon the essential contextual character of "systematic" Christian thought ... is to claim that at its every juncture—in its Christology as in its ethics, in its eschatology as in its *pastoralia*—Christian intellectual reflection entails serious dialogue with the situation of one's world.' D J Hall, *Thinking the Faith: Christian Theology in a North American Context*, Fortress Press, Minneapolis, 1991, 76.

outlined here will be applied in homily or sermon outlines illustrating the practical application of the discussion.

The book will seek to integrate theory and practice by addressing the relationship between a contextual theology of the Holy Land and contextual theology in Britain or the United States. It will then approach the practicalities of translating that contextual theology through the application of appropriate and effective preaching strategies. Each section of the study will involve an enquiry into the impact of the Holy Land upon the preaching of the Gospel in relation to selected sites. In each case the experience of the preacher of pilgrimage is then examined for its wider relevance to preaching in the European or North American context.

The temperament and personal biography as well as experience of the preacher may affect the presentation of the preaching message. For example, a sceptical and reductive mind-set or an over-credulous perspective on the miraculous may have similarly distracting effects on the preaching of miraculous stories in the Gospels. So too, strong prejudices, either in favour of or against particular religious groups or political ideologies, may alienate a pilgrim group or congregation and distort the core message of the preaching. Thus a preacher may have a strong commitment to Jewish-Christian dialogue, which he or she believes might be imperilled by too strong an identification with the Palestinians. Conversely he or she might be so impassioned in favour of the Palestinians that the hearers feel that they are being manipulated in favour of a political agenda that they do not necessarily share.

There is, of course, no way in which the preacher or pilgrim leader can come to a text without presuppositions. What is required, however, is that the preacher will practise an inductive exegesis that will 'involve the preacher in a serious conversation with the text, a conversation that often can and should be shared as part of the sermon.'[2] It will also involve the recognition that inductive 'preaching is and must be a persuasive activity … but it must not be a manipulative one.'[3] Making the same point more vividly Fred Craddock speaks of the ability to get 'alongside the hearers of the Word,'[4] developing a 'methodology that can invite, stimulate, tease, question.' The desired result of this methodology is that the listeners can never be sure whether the central message was something that they heard in the preaching or something that they thought of themselves. Of course, when the preacher is also a pilgrimage group leader, then he or she is quite literally 'alongside

---

[2]   J Webb, *Preaching and the Challenge of Pluralism,* Chalice Press, St Louis, Missouri, 1998, 99.
[3]   *Ibid.,* 57.
[4]   F Craddock, *As One Without Authority,* Chalice Press, St Louis, Missouri, 2001, 56.

the hearers of the Word' on their journey. In this case the test is to empathise sufficiently with the group so as to close the gap between the preacher's thoughts and theirs. In the wider context of the congregation in 'uttermost parts of the earth' the fact that the preacher has visited the Holy Land and discovered or experienced something that illuminates the text, means that the use of such autobiographical material in a homily may be both instructive and persuasive.

It is perhaps appropriate then that I should at this point offer an account of my own experience as a pilgrim and as a preacher of pilgrimage to the Holy Land. I first visited Israel-Palestine in 1981 to participate in a course on 'Palestine in the Time of Jesus' held at St George's College in East Jerusalem. Since then I have been involved in leading and sharing in the leadership of a number of pilgrimages and study tours of the Holy Land, with itineraries covering Jordan, Syria, Israel-Palestine, and the Sinai. I have also been involved actively as chair of a registered British charity promoting the interests of Bir Zeit University, a Palestinian university some eighteen miles north of Jerusalem. I also became convinced of the value of incorporating the human encounter with the peoples and faiths of the Holy Land as a central element in the understanding of Christian pilgrimage to the Holy Land.[5] Most important among such encounters is the meeting with the 'Living Stones',[6] the indigenous Christian communities. Since 1984 the writer has been a committee member of the 'Living Stones Trust', London, and is currently the editor of *Living Stones,* the magazine of the organisation. Living Stones is an ecumenical organisation that seeks to promote links between Christians in the Holy Land and Christians in Britain. Currently it is raising money to provide scholarships to enable Palestinians to train as tour-guides at Bethlehem University.

Such personal involvement with life in the Holy Land and its peoples undoubtedly provide resources for preaching from the preacher's own experience. Writers on homiletics are sharply divided on the value of autobiographical preaching. David Buttrick makes it a point of principle to reject personal illustrations,[7] whereas the essays in the Fleer and Bland symposium, *Preaching Autobiography,* argue strongly for autobiographical

---

[5] A more detailed personal memorandum can be found in the chapter, 'Living Stones and Living Faith', in M Prior, ed., *They Came and They Saw*, Melisende, London, 2000, 57-68.

[6] So called after I Peter 2: 4-5.

[7] 'Though illustrations come to mind in *our* minds and may often be drawn from *our* own experience, we do not have to talk about ourselves in sermons no matter how exhilarating it may be. Personal illustrations always split focus.' D Buttrick, *Homiletic: Moves and Structures*, Fortress Press, Philadelphia, 1987, 143.

preaching.[8] While I do not entirely accept the Fleer and Bland argument, I consider that David Buttrick is wrong to rule such personal preaching out entirely. There are some occasions when the preacher can and should describe his or her own story by way of illustration. In this way the preacher will lead the imagination, understanding and affective judgements of those who hear. Experiences garnered in the Holy Land must often deserve to have a place in such a story. These experiences may be being shared with a pilgrim group in the Holy Land or with a congregation needing to anchor the world of the text into some kind of relationship with their own world. In either case the preacher can use inductive autobiographical preaching as an effective bridge between these two worlds.

Inductive preaching requires a clear idea of who the preacher's hearers are and of their religious, social, and ideological background. Often this will require the recognition, with Leonora Tibbs Tisdale, that preachers 'are struggling to proclaim the Gospel to people whose worlds are different from their own.'[9] Tisdale further suggests: 'One way to bridge the gap is to view preaching as an act of constructing 'local theology'. For the pilgrim group this local theology will need to take account of the physical environment of the Holy Land and the spiritual, political, and social concerns of its people. For those inhabiting 'the uttermost parts of the earth,' local theology will connect with the Holy Land by way of comparison and contrast. Tisdale argues that the community is the author of contextual theology: 'Accommodation to the needs of the congregation mirrors ways of God and exegesis of the congregation is not peripheral.'[10] This may indeed be the case, but contextual theology will only be valid if it is open to the wider local and global context. It is not only preachers who need to open up to their local congregations but local congregations to the world. That is not peripheral either!

The cultural and religious realities of the preacher and of the congregation will influence the way the text is mediated and interpreted.[11] This is evidently the case in the context of Holy Land pilgrimage, too. A pilgrim group that is mainly interested in sightseeing, with a little devotion thrown in, may not be open to a preaching of pilgrimage orientated towards

---

[8] D Fleer, 'Shaped by Story', and C Reed, 'The Promise and Premise of Autobiography for Preaching,' D Fleer, and D Bland, eds., *Preaching Autobiography: Connecting the World of the Preacher to the World of the Text, Rochester College Lectures on Preaching*, Vol. 2, ACU Press, Abilene, Texas, 2001, 23–46 and 97–124.

[9] L Tubbs Tisdale, *Preaching as Local Theology and Folk Art*, Fortress, Minneapolis, 1997, xii.

[10] *Ibid.*, 54.

[11] *Ibid.*, 33.

radical spiritual renewal. Similarly a pilgrim group that is conventionally devotional in its idea of pilgrimage to the Holy Land and has no background or expectation of inter-faith encounter or contextual political theology may experience a culture clash when confronted with these perspectives. At home, too, the preacher with a developed consciousness of inter-faith or political realities in the Holy Land cannot assume the same consciousness in the congregation. It is essential for the preacher or the pilgrimage leader to examine his or her own ethos and experience and compare it with that of congregation before effecting a proper comparative exegesis of the text as illuminated by the religious, social and cultural world of the Holy Land.

For Christians anywhere the world of the Holy Land is the world of the Gospels. Whenever and wherever the Gospel is preached, understanding of that world is an essential part of the background to the text. It is for this reason that pilgrimage to the Holy Land can provide rich insights into that 'world behind the text.' The geography and archaeology of the Holy Land can illuminate the historical background of the Gospel texts. The Holy Land can also shed light on the unfamiliar 'world in front of the text': the complex historical, religious, political, and cultural elements of the Holy Land encountered by the pilgrims who go there today. Sometimes these elements can provide avenues towards the understanding of analogous realities in biblical times. Significantly, however, in today's global village they can also illuminate the preaching context of the world beyond the Holy Land, 'the end of the earth'.

The original setting of most of the Bible, including all of the Gospels and the first thirteen chapters of Acts, is the Holy Land. The term 'Holy Land' here refers primarily to modern Israel-Palestine but can also be widened to include those parts of Jordan, Syria and Egypt that form part of the geographical framework of the biblical narrative.

Holy Land Studies includes within its remit the Holy Land and its surroundings as a geographical and inter-cultural meeting-place. They also include its social history and historiography, pilgrimage to the Holy Land down the ages until today, modern nationalism(s), Western colonialism, the Arab-Israeli conflict, the political economy of Israel-Palestine, state and religion, the role of religion in society, religious and cultural pluralism. To these should be added religion and modernity in the Holy Land, postmodernism and religion, interfaith dialogue(s), interpretation(s) of the Bible and of the Qur'an, and consideration of the relevance of archaeological discourses.[12]

---

[12] M Prior and N Masalha, 'Introducing the Journal', *Holy Land Studies,* Vol. 1, no. 1, Sheffield Academic Press, Sheffield, 2002, 5-7.

Pilgrimage leaders, and by extension, all those engaged in the study of the Holy Land, are in a privileged position for understanding the preaching message. The communication of that message benefits from the historical and critical understanding that the Holy Land can contribute towards the exegesis of the text. Such understanding presents unique opportunities to the preacher because of the richness of background historical and archaeological material provided by the geographical context in which the Gospel was first preached, 'the world behind the text.' However, this material alone cannot dictate the direction of the preaching. Hermeneutical perspectives need to be selected that will take account of the worlds 'in front of the text'. These worlds include the world of the preacher or pilgrimage leader, his or her personal biography with its unique combination of psychological background, social class, theological perspective, personal and political preferences and prejudices. After considering his or her own ethos, the preacher needs, in turn, to engage in an exegesis of the world of the pilgrim group or parish congregation—as well as of the cultural and religious world from which they come.

Finally there is the world to which the preacher and the group or congregation has come, either physically or in the imagination, the world of the Holy Land which exists today as modern Israel-Palestine. This world requires that a hermeneutic be developed that will do justice not only to the Holy Land of the biblical period—the 'world behind the text'—but also to the religious, political, and social realities affecting the peoples living in Israel-Palestine today.[13] This world includes religious, social, and political realities. Some of these realities are continuous with or are, to varying degrees, analogous to the realities of New Testament Palestine. Preaching within the perspective of the Holy Land takes place within the religious context of liturgical, ecumenical, and interfaith realities. It also takes place in an area of contested secular historical and political issues, any or all of which constantly confront the pilgrim or anyone else interpreting the Gospel message against the background of an informed interest in contemporary Israel-Palestine.

It is not always easy for European Christians to acquire the necessary sensitivity for preaching against such a varied, confusing, and frequently challenging background. As Kenneth Cragg has wisely remarked: 'The

---

[13] Edward Said draws attention to the way in which so much of the biblical studies discourse was a feature of Orientalism 'by which Europeans imagined and represented the timeless Orient as they wished to see it not as it was or as its natives believed.' Edward Said, 'Memory, Invention and Space' in I Abu Lughod, *et al.*, eds., *Landscape of Palestine: Equivocal Poetry*, University Publications, Birzeit, West Bank, 1999, 15.

sacrament of geography is too much for our qualities of soul. Feeling becomes either sour or over-indulgent and, in either case, is religiously unreal. A score of temptations await the Christian in the precincts of his redemption and are multiplied again when he takes up his ministries in its meaning to the other religions which in their diversely passionate ways possess the same territories.'[14]

To overcome these temptations requires some knowledge and understanding of the history of the patterns of Christian pilgrimage to the 'precincts of his redemption.' It also requires sensitivity to Christian Ecumenical concerns, Jewish Christian and Muslim Christian dialogue, and an understanding of the volatile and complex realities of the political conflict between Israelis and Palestinians. These realities should also include an understanding of the threat to the survival of the indigenous churches in the Holy Land.[15] Awareness of the 'Living Stones', the local Palestinian Christians, will feed concern at the threat to their survival. In the context of pilgrimage, this concern will express itself in meeting and worshipping with them, including them in the pilgrimage preaching plan, and, where appropriate, in sharing preaching with them in their liturgical celebrations. In the wider preaching context regular references to the existence of Palestinian Christians and to their predicament should result in some effective advocacy on their behalf.

The work addresses the question of how the Gospel message is to be preached and understood within both the classical and the contemporary context of the Holy Land. A number of preaching outlines have been included in this study that are intended to serve as illustrations of the principles that are being presented. Each outline follows a simple preaching plan divided into three 'moves'. These three moves employed here are an adaptation of Eugene Lowry's five stages of narrative plot development (*oops, ugh, aha, whee, and yeah*—or *conflict, complication, sudden shift, good news, and unfolding*[16]). For my chosen simplified version the first move takes a 'life-centred' or 'experience-centred' thematic introduction and leads in to the statement of

---

[14] K Cragg, 'The Anglican Church,' A J Arberry, ed., *Religion in the Middle East*, vol. 1, University Press, Cambridge, 1969, 571.

[15] Although Christian Palestinians make up 6.7 percent of the total of Palestinians throughout the world, the numbers in the West Bank and Gaza now stand at 2.9 percent and in Israel at 2.3 percent in a society that has a 19 percent Palestinian minority. In Jerusalem the Christian population more than halved between 1914 and 1981 and has steadily declined since. M Prior, CM, ed., *They Came and They Saw: Western Christian Experience of the Holy Land*, Melisende, London, 1999, 19, 38-40, and 48.

[16] E Lowry, The Homiletical Plot: The Sermon as Narrative Art Form, Westminster John Knox Press, Atlanta, 1980, 121.

a problematic area which is developed until the second move takes us to a sudden 'reversal' with a declaration of the 'Good News'. The third move attempts to give concrete application of the Gospel message to the lives of the members of the congregation and to link this application to their immediate experience in the Liturgy.

Chapter 1
PREACHING AND PILGRIMAGE TO THE HOLY LAND:
THE EARLY CENTURIES

Now we are going up to Jerusalem, and the Son of Man is about to be handed over
to the chief priests and the scribes. They will condemn him to death and they will
hand him over to the gentiles, who will mock him and spit at him and scourge him
and put him to death and after three days he will rise again (Mark 10: 33-34).

From early times Christians have been drawn to Jerusalem as locus of the death and resurrection of Jesus.[1] The Jews already regarded Jerusalem as the centre of the world, and the mosaic 6th century map of the world at Madaba illustrates that Christians regarded it in the same way.[2] Other places in the Holy Land associated with his birth and his ministry also claimed a place in the Christian imagination.

All liturgy and liturgical preaching takes place within or creates sacred place.[3] The Holy Land of what is today Israel-Palestine has its special claim to be regarded as sacred space. As the locus of the events, real or imagined, recorded in the Old Testament, Jerusalem and other sacred places of the Holy Land had an established importance within Judaism. Until the destruction of the Second Temple, pilgrimage was a compulsory feature of Judean religion. For Muslims the pilgrimage to Mecca, the *Hajj*, one of the five pillars of Islam. By contrast, for Christians, visiting the holy places in Palestine has always been optional. However, long before the institution of Christian pilgrimage to the Holy Land had become generally established,

---

[1] Certainly, the practice of praying at these places had become established by the fourth century, and there is evidence that it goes back well before that date and has continued up until today. H Chadwick, *The Circle and the Ellipse: Rival Concepts of Authority in the Early Church,* Inaugural Lecture, Oxford University Press, 1959, 7.

[2] J Wilkinson, *Jerusalem Pilgrimages Before the Crusades,* Aris and Philips, Warminster, 2002, 53.

[3] The *locus classicus* of the theme of sacred space is M Eliade, *Sacred and Profane,* trans. W R Trask, Harcourt Brace and World Inc., New York, 1959, Chapter V, 'Sacred Space and making the World Sacred'.

the geographical locations associated with the life of Jesus, in particular Jerusalem, had seminal importance.[4]

Preaching was from the first an important feature of Christian pilgrimage to the Holy Land and the Holy Land was to develop a correspondingly important role in preaching. However, it was not only the need to inform the imagination that drew Christians towards the land of Jesus. A survey of the history of Christian pilgrimage to the Holy Land over the centuries reveals that pilgrims have been driven by a variety of spiritual motives. These include desire for closer sense of communion with God, for reparation for sin, and to express thanksgiving or to pray for a particular intention.

Pilgrimage to the Holy Land can also be understood in political, cultural or economic terms as a mechanism for establishing influence or control in the region or for exporting internal contradictions from the pilgrims' own society. Whatever the reasons or explanations given for going on pilgrimage to the Holy Land, however, actual pilgrimage invariably includes one or more of the four elements of historical enquiry, devotional imagination, liturgy, and preaching.

The presence and the relative importance of these four appears variously in the earliest accounts with their various emphases upon prayer and Bible reading at holy sites, participation in the worship of the Jerusalem Church, and listening to preaching. Some, if not all the four, also reappear in later mediaeval pilgrimage, the didactic 19th century form of Protestant pilgrimage, and the later devotional pilgrimage of Eastern Orthodox pilgrims. The importance of the indigenous Christian communities for foreign pilgrims has not always been recognised, and in the next chapter there will be some discussion of the value of sharing in the liturgy and preaching of these communities and a record of some experiences of such sharing.

In 323 the Emperor Constantine made Christianity the official religion of the Roman empire. His mother Helena visited Palestine and took considerable interest in identifying biblical sites. In particular she began the building of the Church of the Holy Sepulchre, believed to enclose the sites of the crucifixion, death, and burial of Jesus.[5] The available records of pilgrimage before that suggest it was primarily the spirit of historical enquiry

---

[4] Numerous instances in New Testament and the pre-Nicene Fathers where the Land of Promise and the Holy City become symbols for a spiritual eschatology are catalogued in chapter 3 of R Wilken, *The Land Called Holy: Palestine in Christian History and Thought*, Yale University Press, Newhaven and London, 1992, 46-64.

[5] As early as 160 evidence of Melito of Sardis identified the rock of Golgotha as by then 'in the middle of the city.' In view of this testimony Wilkinson considers 'to doubt that this rock marks the place of the Cross flies against available evidence.' Wilkinson, *op. cit.*, 63.

that motivated pilgrims before the time of Constantine, although preaching seems to have figured in their stories also. Other less educated pilgrims may have had other ideas about the meaning of the holy sites but in the nature of things they have left no literary record.

The earliest recorded Christian pilgrim to the Holy Land was Melito of Sardis (d.190), a pilgrim whose interest in the Holy Land involved the two elements of historical enquiry and preaching. His theological opposition to Gnosticism probably inspired his visit to the Holy Land in around 160. Since the Gnostics denied both the physical humanity of Christ and the unity of the Old and New Testament dispensations, it was important for Melito to establish accurately the books of the Old Testament and to identify the scenes of the Lord's incarnate life.

Another pre-Constantinian pilgrim to the Holy Land was the Alexandrine theologian and philosopher Origen (c.185-254). While still a layman Origen went to Palestine in 215 to preach at the invitation of the bishops of Caesarea and Aelia (Jerusalem). Recalled to Alexandria by his bishop, Origen later returned to Palestine in 230, setting up a school of theology at Caesarea in 231. In his travels around the Holy Land one of his primary concerns was to seek out the sites of biblical events.[6] According to Firmilianus, a Cappadocian bishop who visited Origen there, he was in the Holy Land for the sake of the holy places, and in particular, to trace the footsteps of Jesus.[7] While in Jerusalem, Origen studied Hebrew and debated with Jewish scholars, developing his thesis that 'when the Scriptures speak of Jerusalem they do not have in mind the city in Judea that was once the capital of the Jewish nation. Jerusalem ... does not designate a future political center but a spiritual vision of heavenly bliss.'[8]

It seems evident that Melito and Origen both went to the Holy Land for scholarly rather than for spiritual reasons. Thus one commentator claims that it is 'misleading, indeed anachronistic, to call Origen a pilgrim'.[9] Clearly, Jerusalem did not have the same significance for them as for later pilgrims. Indeed, at this stage, it was Caesarea rather than Aelia (Jerusalem) that had the chief bishop of Palestine, and 'Jerusalem had no special place on the Christian map.'[10] Nonetheless, it seems that the Mount of Olives, the

---

[6] 'Origen's interest was as much historical and exegetical as it was religious.' Wilken, *op. cit.*, 108.

[7] E D Hunt, *Holy Land Pilgrimage in the Later Roman Empire AD 312-460*, Clarendon Press, Oxford, 1984, 4.

[8] Wilken, *op. cit.*, 76.

[9] *Ibid.*, 108.

[10] K Armstrong, *A History of Jerusalem: One City Three Faiths,* HarperCollins, London, 1996, 171.

Garden of Gethsemane, and the River Jordan had a devotional significance for the Christians who lived in Aelia. With their focus on the heavenly Jerusalem rather than the earthly one, the Christians of this period would view Jerusalem from the Mount of Olives and meditate upon its rejection of the Lord rather than upon its status as a holy city. On the Mount of Olives too, they visited and prayed at a cave that was, reputedly, the site of a resurrection appearance to John the Beloved Disciple.[11] At nearby Bethlehem, they venerated the cave of the Nativity.

Eusebius, Bishop of Caesarea, narrates the story of the visits of Melito and Origen but did not then discern any special significance for geographical Palestine. In Eusebius's anti-Judaism polemics he frequently contrasts Jerusalem with the heavenly city or with the new Roman City of Aelia Capitolina built on the site of Herodian Jerusalem. The ideal of a Christian Jerusalem was so new and so little rooted in Christian piety that Eusebius could make no place for it in his disputes with the Jews. In his later writings, however, the restoration of the Holy Sepulchre was to elicit a much more positive attitude. Certainly, the holy places became more valued as an orthodox reaction to the Arian Christology with which Eusebius sympathised.

If the Incarnate Word was indeed fully God, then the points of contact between the Word and the physical world became vitally important. In his 'Letter 108 to Eustocium,' St Jerome describes the extraordinary fervour of two aristocratic Roman women, Paula and her daughter, as they venerated the sacred sites in Jerusalem.[12] The Orthodox reaction to the Arian heresy helps to explain the emergence of such fervent veneration of the material locations where the Divine Word had intersected with the human world. Consequent upon the conversion of Constantine to Christianity, the holy places of Palestine also served an ideological purpose by attracting pilgrims to the Holy Land and thus consolidating both the influence of the new faith and the authority of the emperor who espoused it.

Even among the Orthodox, however, the practice of pilgrimage did not go unchallenged. Gregory of Nyssa, writing in 379 AD,[13] attacks pilgrimage

---

[11] Hunt, *op. cit.*, 121-2.

[12] We read that she 'fell down and worshipped before the Cross as if she could see the Lord hanging on it. On entering the Tomb of the Resurrection she kissed the stone which the angel removed from the sepulchre door; then like a thirsty man who has waited long, and at last comes to water, she faithfully kissed the very shelf on which the Lord's body had lain. Her tears and lamentations there are known to all Jerusalem—or rather to the Lord himself to whom she was praying.' Wilken, *op. cit.*, 121.

[13] Gregory of Nyssa, *Life of Holy Macrina*, ed. Ducaeus/Gretser, *Patrologia Graeca* 46, tr. H O Ogle, *Nicene and Post Nicene Fathers*, Oxford University Press, Oxford, 1890-1900.

on the grounds that it was not enjoined in the New Testament, it encouraged a dangerous mixing of the sexes, and it brought people no closer to God. In any case, his Church in his native Cappadocia had more to recommend it than did the Church in Jerusalem. Elsewhere, however, Gregory is defending the sacramental and incarnational character of orthodox Christianity and asserts that the Holy Land had special significance for Christian believers because it has the 'signs of the Lord's sojourn in the flesh'[14] and 'received the footprints of Life itself.'[15]

One of the first of the increasing number of pilgrims who left any record of their journey was the Bordeaux Pilgrim (died c. 333), whose account amounts to little more than a catalogue of biblical sites. There is no reference to prayer or liturgical celebration as a feature of his pilgrimage or of any contact with local Christians.

The most important record of pilgrimage during this period is that of Egeria (381-384), who was probably a nun, who travelled to holy places throughout the Middle East. She records liturgical celebrations with preaching in Jerusalem[16] and elsewhere and, although the Eucharist was not a feature of her visits to the shrines outside the basilicas in Jerusalem, that visits to the other sites were always accompanied by the reading of the appropriate biblical text. The preaching in Jerusalem was preceded by sermons from those presbyters who wished to preach. In consequence the service which had begun at daybreak did not conclude until ten or eleven o'clock. The object of all this preaching, Egeria explains, 'is to make sure that the people will continually be learning about the Bible and the love of God.'[17] Similar multiple sermons were available on Wednesday afternoons in Lent.[18]

It is clear from our brief survey of early Christian pilgrimage that a major concern was to visit the places associated with the Bible and the ministry of Jesus. In the case of Egeria in particular, we have detailed accounts of her participation in the liturgical ceremonies in Jerusalem, and of the preaching of the Bishop of Jerusalem. She describes her participation in the Sunday and daily offices of Morning and Evening Prayer,[19] participation in

---

[14] *Vita Macrinae*, pref. (*Patrologia Graecae*, 46, 9060a); ep. 3 Pasquali, 21.

[15] Ep. 3.4, Pasquali, 21.

[16] 'It is clear that Egeria found a much greater emphasis on preaching about the Scriptures in the regular Sunday Eucharists than she had been accustomed to ... .' E D Hunt, *Holy Land Pilgrimage in the Later Roman Empire AD 312-460*, Clarendon Press, Oxford, 1984.

[17] J Wilkinson, *Egeria's Travels, Newly translated with supporting documents*, Aris and Philips, Warminster, 1999, 145.

[18] *Ibid.*, 149.

[19] *Ibid.*, 143-4.

the Holy Week Ceremonies, including a procession of palms from the Mount of Olives on Palm Sunday[20] and the veneration of the Cross on Good Friday.[21] She also gives accounts of her worship at Pentecost,[22] the Presentation,[23] and the Feast of the Epiphany at the Church of the Nativity in Bethlehem.[24] She also refers to the use of appropriate prayers and readings accompanying her visits to other holy places.[25]

Throughout the Byzantine period established pilgrimage itineraries developed.[26] Pilgrims also collected or purchased relics and sacred souvenirs of earth, cloth, water, and stones. Major relics were also removed to Constantinople and elsewhere so as to provide regional pilgrimage centres. At the same time hermits and ascetics flocked to Palestine and surrounding areas to set up hermitages and, in due course, monasteries that in turn became shrines of their sanctified mortal remains.[27] Shrines built over supposed holy sites multiplied, and pilgrims took the opportunity to join in liturgical celebrations at these shrines, often joining with the indigenous faithful. It is noteworthy too that it was the indigenous faithful who identified and developed most of the pilgrimage sites.[28] Sharing in the Holy Week and Easter celebrations at Jerusalem and in the Christmas feast at Bethlehem was particularly popular. These events provided ample opportunity for highly-charged liturgical preaching as is evident in the sermons of Cyril of Jerusalem, the first Bishop of Jerusalem to preside at the Liturgy in the Church of the Holy Sepulchre.[29] The volume of preaching

---

[20] *Ibid.*, 151.

[21] *Ibid.*, 155.

[22] *Ibid.*, 159-61

[23] *Ibid.*, 147-8.

[24] *Ibid.*, 146-7

[25] 'And it was always our practice when we managed to reach one of the places we wanted to see, to have first a prayer, then a reading from the book, then to say an appropriate psalm and another prayer. By God's grace we always followed this practice whenever we were able to reach a place we wanted to see.' *Ibid.*, 120.

[26] By the 7th century, in addition to the principal churches of interest in and around Jerusalem, pilgrimages had also come to include Bethany, Bethlehem, and Nazareth. *Pilgrimage*, C Mango, ed., *The Oxford History of Byzantium,* Oxford University Press, Oxford, 2002, 115.

[27] *Ibid.*, 115 and 209.

[28] 'It is only from the residents of Palestine that we can discern the lineaments of an emerging Christian idea of a holy land.' Wilken, *op. cit.*, 119.

[29] 'In sermons preached in the basilica ... Cyril took full advantage of his unparalleled setting ... "others hear but we both see and touch" ' (cat. 13.22). Others have received the testimony of the prophets concerning the Lord, but only Christians in Jerusalem have the witness of holy places.' Wilken, *op. cit.*, 119.

material originating from Jerusalem suggests frequent if not daily preaching at the Church of the Holy Sepulchre.[30]

Internal evidence from the sermons of Hesychius of Jerusalem (c. 380–445) on Job suggest that they were preached at the Church of the Upper Room, possibly during Lent at weekday Eucharists on Wednesdays and Fridays.[31] Hesychius was not a bishop, an ecclesiastical politician, or a theological controversialist but is remembered exclusively for his outstanding preaching in the tradition of classical rhetoric.[32] His verse by verse exposition of the book of Job was clearly intended for a mixed congregation that would have included ordinary pilgrims and local lay people as well as clergy and ascetics.

During the Byzantine period Palestine had became a centre of pilgrimage for Christians from all over the world. Unfortunately relations with the Jewish minority community were marked by mutual hostility. Christian rule was suspended between 361–363 during the reign of Emperor Julian the Apostate. He renounced the Christian faith and encouraged the Jews to rebuild the Temple. According to tradition, the work was destroyed by an earthquake and, on Julian's death, the project ended. This episode encouraged anti-Jewish feeling among Christians, and Julian's successor Jovian excluded Jews from Jerusalem.

The Emperor Justinian, who ruled from 527 to 565, initiated major building projects. These included the rebuilding of the Church of the Nativity at Bethlehem and the erection of the Church of the Holy Theotokos (Mother of God, a title of the Virgin Mary) on Mount Sion. He also enacted further measures against the Jews.

In 614 the Persians invaded the eastern Byzantine empire, occupying Palestine, destroying churches and murdering Christian monks and hermits. More than sixty thousand Christians were massacred and the Church of the Holy Sepulchre destroyed. The Church of the Nativity in Bethlehem apparently survived on account of the Persian dress and apparel of the magi

---

[30] 'By the beginning of the fifth century, Jerusalem still had regular, daily expository preaching … . That this should happen in the Jerusalem is no surprise. The Gospels tell us that Jesus taught daily in the Temple and Acts tells us that the apostles did the same thing. By the fifth century the Temple was long gone, but we can well imagine that there was daily preaching at the Church of the Holy Sepulchre, which was where the pilgrims would more than likely gather … .' H O Old, *The Reading and Preaching of the Scriptures in the Worship of the Christian Church. Vol. 2, The Patristic Age*, Eerdmans, Grand Rapids, Michigan, and Cambridge, England, 1998, 128.

[31] *Ibid.*, 129. Old bases this argument on research published in Charles Renoux, *Hesychius of Jerusalem, Homelies sur Job* (Armenian text with French translation), *'Patrologies Orientalis'*, vol. 42, Turnhout, Brepols, 1938.

[32] *Ibid.*, 125 and 133.

painted on the pillars of the Church. According to one authority, the monk Antiochus Strategos, the Jews were put in charge of Jerusalem and helped in the massacres. In 628 the Byzantines re-conquered Palestine and the Jewish population was expelled.

Exhausted by the war with the Persians, the Byzantines were unable to resist the armies of the new faith of Islam, and in 638 Caliph 'Umar took Jerusalem peacefully and allowed the Jews to return. For more than three hundred years the Holy Land had been sacred space for Byzantine Christianity. The intolerance shown towards dissident Christians and the followers of Judaism may have contributed to the downfall of this part of the Byzantine empire. From 638 onwards, however, the context of pilgrimage and the role of the Holy Land in Christian preaching and imagination would never be the same. The Holy Land would thereafter be contested territory between three religions, and most of the recorded Christian discourse and preaching about the Holy Land, with the exception of the period of Crusader rule, would be predominantly from the perspective of exile.

Preaching Plan: Mark 14: 12-16, 22-26,[33]
the Institution of the Eucharist
Preparation of the Homily: Process and Strategies

The text from Mark is that which is appointed for the Gospel reading in year B for *Corpus Christi* (The solemnity for the Body and Blood of Christ). However, since this homily is primarily mystagogical rather than exegetical, it could have been used with minor alteration with the other readings appointed for Corpus Christi in years A and C or with the Lucan or Matthean parallels.

---

[33] Mark 14: 12-16, 22-26: On the first day of Unleavened Bread, when the Passover lamb was sacrificed, his disciples said to Jesus, 'Where do you want us to go and make the preparations for you to eat the Passover?' So he sent two of his disciples, saying to them, 'Go into the city and you will meet a man carrying a pitcher of water. Follow him, and say to the owner of the house which he enters, "The Master says: Where is my dining room in which I can eat the Passover with my disciples?" He will show you a large upper room furnished with couches, all prepared. Make the preparations for us there.' The disciples set out and went to the city and found everything as he had told them, and prepared the Passover.

And as they were eating he took some bread, and when he had said the blessing he broke it and gave it to them. 'Take it,' he said 'this is my body.' Then he took a cup, and when he had returned thanks he gave it to them, and all drank from it, and he said to them, 'This is my blood, the blood of the covenant, which is to be poured out for many. I tell you solemnly, I shall not drink any more wine until the day I drink the new wine in the kingdom of God.'

It could also be preached at the Franciscan Church of the Cenacle, adjacent to the traditional site of the Last Supper. In fact the 'playing with the idea' stage of reflection drew insights from the immediate environment of the Cenacle and its associations in a way that points to the value of the experience of pilgrimage to the Holy Land for the diaspora preacher.

The value in this case relates both to the inter-faith associations on Mount Sion and to the reminder of genocide and inhumanity provided by the nearby Chamber of the Holocaust. Each of these provides opportunities to explore wider dimensions in reflecting upon the mystery of the Eucharist. Immediately behind the Franciscan Church is the Cenacle, which once formed part of the same Franciscan monastic complex. The Cenacle is on the site of the church built by Maximos, Bishop of Caesarea, in the early part of the 4th century. Maximos built the church around what he believed to be the Upper Room where Jesus instituted the Eucharist and where the disciples received the Holy Spirit at Pentecost. This was then 'The birthplace of the Church and the Mother of all other Churches.'[34] The room today is a Crusader chapel converted into a mosque by the Ottomans in 1556 and designated Masjid al-Nabi Da'ud (the mosque of the prophet David).

Part of the same complex has, since 1948, included a Jewish King David Museum, supposedly including the tomb of David and, nearby, the 'Chamber of the Holocaust' which doubles as a museum of anti-semitism and a memorial to six million victims of the *Shoah*. This last includes a bar of soap made from human fat. The juxtaposition of this gruesome reminder of how the dignity of the human body can be degraded has been used as powerful homiletic counterpoint to the mystery of the sacramental Body of Christ celebrated a few yards away. [35]

Homily Outline
PROBLEMATIC

Not far from the traditional place where Jesus celebrated the Last Supper with his disciples is a museum commemorating the crimes committed against the Jews in Europe during the Second World War. This place has some horrific reminders about how the human body has been abused and degraded by human wickedness. Of course, the great atrocity committed against the Jews surpasses other atrocities in its scale, but it takes it

---

[34] K Armstrong, *Jerusalem, One City, Three Faiths*, HarperCollins, London, 1996, 190.

[35] The inspiration for this homiletic linkage between the soap in the Chamber of the Holocaust and the Body of Christ was first suggested to me from reading Hubert Richards, 'Thoughts on a Journey', *Scripture Bulletin*, Vol. 5, num. 2, Winter 1974–5, Catholic Biblical Association of Great Britain, London, 33.

place alongside other great historic evils committed against the dignity of human beings. Dresden, Hiroshima, Cambodia, and Rwanda immediately come to mind. It also takes its place alongside smaller-scale massacres. The killing of Palestinians by Israeli snipers or missiles or the killing of Israeli civilians by suicide bombers does not amount to an Auschwitz or a Hiroshima, but it is no less terrible for the individual victims and those who mourn them. Human bodies are torn and mangled. Human blood is spilt over dirt tracks and pavements. We may reflect also that there are other ways in which human bodies are degraded. They are degraded by starvation and neglect—by physical and sexual abuse. There are so many ways in which humanity denies the dignity of the bodies God has given to us.

Good News

And on the night before he was betrayed Jesus took the bread and said, 'This is my Body.' His Body too, would be abused, tortured, and done to death, but it would also be raised up and taken into glory. This is good news because he took his human nature from us, so as to enable us to share in his victory, to become the Body of Christ. A short distance from the Cenacle on Mount Sion is the Church of the Dormition commemorating Our Lady's journey from this life to share body and soul in the victory of her Son. And Mary represents us. We too can hope to share in his victory. And the victory is not just for us as isolated individuals. Holy Communion is not just a sign that I am united with Jesus Christ. It is also a sign of the unity of the Church. It is a sign of unity that can stand against the violence and divisions that degrade and destroy the bodies of men and women.

Application to Liturgy and Life

So when we ask how this affects our lives and our world, we remember that all those who share in the Body and Blood of the Lord share in the one bread and the one cup. The room of the Last Supper on Mount Sion in Jerusalem was used for several centuries as a Muslim shrine, and nearby there is the Jewish 'Tomb of David.' This reminds me that there is a need for a unity that embraces not only Christians but everyone. The Eucharist is a sign for Christians—that Christians are called to be one. It can also be a sign that serves to remind us of the wider unity that God wills for all the people on earth—one family, one body, and one blood.

Whoever we are, whether our bodies are healthy or sick, beautiful or ugly, young or old, broken down or fighting fit—they are the Body of Christ destined to share in his glory. 'This is my Body,' says Jesus. At the preparation of the gifts, we can think of the bread and wine that are brought up as representing us—our souls and our bodies. Jesus will take them and say, 'This is my Body. This is my Blood.' For this reason we must value our bodies as well as those of others. We must not degrade them or damage them. And we must campaign for a world where people are valued and where bodies are treated with respect—a world where there are no sick or hungry people, a world without violence and war. Those who share in the body and blood of Christ in the Eucharist have a responsibility to work for the unity of all humanity. Those who worship Jesus Christ in the Eucharist in his sacramental presence have a responsibility to care for his Body in the world and to work for the unity of all.

Chapter 2
CHRISTIAN PILGRIMAGE FROM THE ARAB CONQUEST UNTIL TODAY

May my tongue remain stuck to my palate if I do not keep you in mind, if I do not count Jerusalem the greatest of my joys (Psalm 137).

Spiritually authentic Christian pilgrimage to the Holy Land requires the three elements of historical enquiry, liturgy and preaching. In the history of pilgrimage one or more of these three elements has too often been left out. A fourth element of the drive towards political and cultural hegemony over the Holy Land and its people needs to be displaced by an essential commitment to encounter between the pilgrim liturgical community and that of the 'Living Stones of the Land'.

With the coming of Islam in 638 Christian pilgrimage persisted, and the indigenous Christians enjoyed a measure of real, if unequal freedom.[1] Christians were allowed to restore their churches, and the 7th and 8th centuries 'saw quite a spate of church building in Syria and Palestine.'[2]

Christian pilgrimage to the Holy Land continued and the experience of pilgrims was fed back to the nations from which they came. In the late 7th century, Arculf, a bishop of Gaul, went to the Holy Land, and Adomnan, who was Abbot of Iona (679-704), recorded an account of his pilgrimage. Bede praised this work as of value to those 'who can know the holy places only through what they learn from books.'[3] We have documentary memoirs from other western pilgrims in the 8th and 9th centuries: the English St Willibald (700-86) and the monk Fidelis whose tour of the sites of the Holy Land and Egypt was recorded by the Irish monk Dicuil (b. 760).[4] The Emperor Charlemagne was one of the most powerful pilgrims to worship at the Holy Sepulchre. He established good relations with the Caliph Harun al-Rashid who ruled from 786 to 809. Harun allowed him to adorn holy

---

[1] The decree or 'covenant' sometimes ascribed to Caliph 'Umar, the Muslim conqueror of Jerusalem as reported by Patriarch Eutychius of Alexandria, writing in the tenth century, reads as follows: 'In the Name of God the Merciful and the Lord of Mercy. From 'Umar ibn Khattab to the citizens of Aelia, They shall have security for their lives, their children, their goods, and their churches, which shall neither be pulled down nor occupied.' J Wilkinson, *Jerusalem Pilgrimages Before the Crusades*, Aris and Phillips, Westminster, 2002, 17.
[2] K Armstrong, *A History of Jerusalem. One City Three Faiths,* HarperCollins, London, 1996, 232.
[3] Wilkinson, *op cit.*, 18.
[4] *Ibid.*, 22-23.

places in Jerusalem and Bethlehem and gave him honorary guardianship of the Holy Sepulchre. Charlemagne also founded a church, a library, and a hospice opposite the *Anastasis,* or shrine of the resurrection.[5] This last is recorded in the pilgrimage diary of Bernard the Monk who stayed there when he visited Jerusalem seventy years later.[6] The motives for pilgrimage to the Holy Land during this period are summed up by Eutychius of Alexandria. Eutychius saw the holy places as a foretaste of heavenly reward: 'By these relics and places … Christ gave us, all joined in one, a blessing, a sanctification, an approach to him, pardon for sins, feasts in which men come together in his name, spiritual joy without end, and witnesses confirming the Scriptures.'[7]

From the time of the Ikshidid dynasty (915-969) onwards, there were a number of lapses in the previously generally tolerant attitude of Muslim rulers. The years between 923 and 944 saw a series of successful campaigns by the Byzantine general John Kourkuas. In 938 Muslim mobs attacked the Christian Palm Sunday procession and set light to the gates of the Martyrion. Subsequent riots saw more attacks on Christian holy sites and the burning alive of the Patriarch John who had unwisely called upon the Byzantines to liberate Jerusalem. In the next century things became even worse for the Christians under the Fatimid Caliph Hakim, 'the mad,' who destroyed the Church of the Holy Sepulchre, in 1009. After the disappearance of Hakim in 1021, chaos ensued until Fatimid Caliph al-Zahir established control in 1029. Al-Zahir inaugurated a period of rebuilding in Jerusalem and a restoration of relations with Byzantium. The Church of the Holy Sepulchre was rebuilt in 1048 at Byzantine imperial expense, and by 1063 the Christians had been granted a secure Christian Quarter in the area around the Holy Sepulchre. At the same time the number of Armenian pilgrims led to the development of an Armenian Quarter nearby, to the south west of the city.

Despite the dangers involved, Christian pilgrims, fuelled by millennial expectations linked with the end of the first millennium, continued coming to the Holy Land. Such pilgrims as came to the Holy Land were inspired chiefly by a powerful devotion, making them ready to risk persecution and danger. With the normalisation of conditions in the 1030s, the number of pilgrims increased still more.[8] Rodulf Glaber, a French monk from Cluny

---

[5] Armstrong, *op cit.,* 252.

[6] Wilkinson, *op cit.,* 24-5.

[7] *Ibid.,* 75.

[8] 'When the end of days failed to occur, people began to wonder whether 1033, the thousandth anniversary of the crucifixion, was a more appropriate date.' *Ibid.,* 267.

who came to Jerusalem around 1030, describes the phenomenon: 'From all over the world an innumerable crowd began to flock to the Sepulchre of the Saviour in Jerusalem—in greater numbers than any one had before thought possible. Not only were there some of the common people and of the middle class, but there were several very great kings, counts and noblemen. Finally—and this had never happened before—many noble ladies set out with the poor people. Many desired that they might die rather than return home.'[9]

There then followed a train of events that led to a new kind of military pilgrimage—the Crusade. In 1064, Bishop Arnold of Bamberg led an ostentatiously wealthy pilgrimage to the Holy Land which was robbed and massacred by Bedouin bands. In 1071, the Seljuk Turks defeated the Byzantines at the Battle of Manzikert, and the eastern Byzantine frontier collapsed. The western response to the Byzantine emperor's appeal for help combined a desire to ensure the protection of Christian pilgrims with the wish to re-establish Christian control over the holy places.

In 1099 the Crusaders took Jerusalem and established western Christian hegemony over the region until their first loss of Jerusalem in 1187 and their final expulsion from the region, after the fall of Acre in 1291. During this period Christian pilgrimage to the Holy Land was clearly dominated by a combination of militant Christian devotion and a desire for political and military control.[10] Both forces worked to produce a strong emphasis on the Holy Land in the western Christian imagination with consequent impact upon preaching and devotion.

According to the Crusader leader Robert of Reims, Jerusalem was the 'navel of the world.' Not only was it from there that the Christian religion had its beginnings, it was also to be the site of the Second Coming of Christ and of the Final Judgement.[11] Crusading became an admired commitment to a life of penance in accordance with the mood of the time.[12] The Council

---

[9] Wilkinson, *op. cit.*, 272.

[10] It can be argued that this combination of the devotional and the political-military elements was also present in earlier Byzantine adventures aiming to recover Byzantine control of the Holy Land, the 'ersatz' crusade of Tzimisces in 975 being the best example. Historical evidence concerning the precise purpose and execution of this 'Crusade' is disputed, however. G Regan, *First Crusade, Byzantium's Holy Wars*, Sutton, London, 2001, 208-16.

[11] N Housley, *The Crusaders*, Tempus, London, 2002, 17.

[12] 'The most important expression of the renewed spirituality in the eleventh century—which originated in Cluny—was the penitential pilgrimage. Conceived as a penance in the wake of contrition, the pilgrimage became a meritorious act for the pious or the repentant sinner. The novelty of the eleventh century revival lay in characterizing pilgrimage as an act of collective expiation ... Pilgrimage to holy shrines changed from

of Clermont pronounced, 'Whoever for devotion only, not to gain honour or money, goes to Jerusalem, to liberate the Church of God can substitute this journey for all penance.'[13]

During the Crusader period interest in the historical also re-emerged. Old shrines were restored and new shrines were discovered providing new homiletic and liturgical opportunities, and local alternative Holy Land sites developed. Although preaching was not a regular or even a frequent feature of mediaeval worship, Latin bishops and the members of preaching orders could now hone their homiletic skills and motivate volunteers to 'take the cross.'

Preaching aimed at promoting the Crusades is an important feature in the history of Christian homiletics. Although it is difficult to separate actual texts of sermons from literary accounts of them, Urban II, Peter the Hermit, Jacques of Vitry, Fulk of Nueilly, and St Bernard of Clairvaux[14] were among the best-known preachers to use their rhetorical skills to this end. Such preaching was a turning point in both the purpose and the manner of preaching.[15] It also served both to emphasise the importance of the Holy Land for the devotional imagination and, unfortunately, to whip up ignorant prejudice against Muslims branded as 'pagans' and pogroms against the Jews as enemies of Christ nearer to home.[16]

The importance of the role of preaching in the context of the Crusades themselves is testified to by the preaching mission of Jacques of Vitry (c. 1170-1240). Jacques' accompanied the soldiers on the Fifth Crusade,

---

an act of individual piety to one of collective penance. Hundreds of people from all stations of life—both clergy and laity—assembled for common pilgrimages, some directed to the Holy Land.' Joshua Prawer, *The Crusaders' Kingdom: European Colonialism in the Middle Ages*, Phoenix Press, London, 2001 (hardback edition, Praeger, New York, 1972), 205-7.

[13] *Ibid.*, 177.

[14] Bernard's preaching of the Crusades has been described as 'one of the triumphs of Christian oratory'. H O Old, *The Reading and Preaching of the Scriptures in the Worship of the Christian Church*, Volume 3, *The Medieval Church*, Eerdmans, Grand Rapids, Michigan, and Cambridge, England, 1999, 256. Bernard was responsible for preaching the Crusade to a huge crowd of people at Vélzalay in Burgundy in the Holy Week of 1146. Subsequently he went on to preach the Crusade in cities all over Burgundy, Flanders, and the Rhineland.

[15] Old, *op. cit.*, 338.

[16] A sermon attributed to a Crusader preacher by Baldric of Bourgeuil: 'I address you fathers and sons, brothers and nephews. If an outsider were to strike any of your kin down would you not avenge your blood relative? How much more ought you to avenge your God, your father, your brother, whom you see reproached, banished from his estates, crucified.' N Housley, *op. cit.*, 25.

and his preaching reminded them of the higher purpose of the Crusades and the rewards that awaited them in heaven.[17] Jacques' earthly reward came earlier, and he was made Bishop of Acre in 1216. However, preaching was only one of the ways in which the Bible stories were made to come alive for the pilgrims of this period. The interest in the historical involved the rebuilding of abandoned Byzantine shrines as well as the development of new ones, responding to the enlargement or loss of territory.[18] Alternative pilgrimage itineraries from Acre were developed. The first went across to Tiberias and then through Samaria and Judaea to Jerusalem, and the second went south along the coast and then inland to Jerusalem. By the middle of the 13th century the 'holy and legendary geography of the Holy Land was minutely fixed until modern research played havoc with this charming canvas of credulity.'[19] In Jerusalem, in particular, the identification of these sites meant that festivals could be celebrated and the events they commemorated re-enacted in what was, supposedly, their original historical setting. Joshua Prawer remarks that one 13th-century text [20] offers insights into 'a world where history and geography rub shoulders with mediaeval exegesis, folklore and the most improbable identification sites.'[21] Since Acre itself lacked other biblical associations it was identified with the Old Testament Ekron, but what it 'lacked in biblical memories was offset by the profusion of indulgences accorded to visiting pilgrims.'[22] In view of the hostility of the Crusaders to Islam and Judaism, it is paradoxical that some of the shrines that became popular with the western Christian pilgrims enjoyed shared associations with Judaism and/or Islam.[23] Following the Western custom, since Mass would be celebrated daily and not be limited to Sundays and feast days, pilgrims might assist at Mass at all of these shrines. Apart from the holy shrines, the festivities

---

[17] Old, *op. cit.*, 335.

[18] One example is the relocation of Emmaus to safer ground, referred to on p. 36.

[19] Prawer, *op. cit.*, 176.

[20] 'Pelerinages et Pardounes de Acre', in T Tobler and A Molinier, eds., *Itinera Hierosolymtiana et descriptions Terrae Sanctae bellis sacris anteriora et latina lingua exarata,* I, 1-2 vols., Geneva 1972, and Vol. II, A Molinier and C Kohler, Geneva, 1885. T Tobler, *Descriptiones Terrae Sanctae ex saec.,* VIII, IX, XII, XV, Leipzig, 1874.

[21] Prawer, *op. cit.,* 205.

[22] *Ibid.*, 213.

[23] Examples include the tomb of Abraham in Hebron, the tomb of David on Mount Sion, the 'Cave of the Lion' in the cemetery of the canons of the Holy Sepulchre (Mamillah) near the Jaffa Gate—scene of a miraculous intervention by a lion to rescue Christians/Jews from Persians/Christians who were casting them into the flames, 'Ain Baqar, near to Acre, where Adam first ploughed the land, the Green Mosque (Al-Khadra) in Ascalon, which became Sta Maria Cathara, the cave of Elijah on Carmel, the Temple Mount and the Mount of Olives. *Ibid.,* 185.

of the Christian calendar were the greatest attraction for pilgrims from abroad. Feasts included a procession from the Holy Sepulchre to the site of the event commemorated.

Other festivals commemorated more recent events such as the anniversary of the capture of Jerusalem and the consecration of the restored Church of the Holy Sepulchre. The celebration of the first of these took the form of a procession from the Church of the Holy Sepulchre to the *Templum Domini*, the title given by the Crusaders to the Dome of the Rock which they had converted into a church. The route of the procession went along the outside walls to the place where the Crusaders had broken through in 1099 before spreading massacre and mayhem on their way to the Holy Sepulchre. Here the procession would stop, and a commemorative sermon would be preached.[24] This is one example of different linguistic groups making such preaching problematic since although one 'could participate in the liturgy with little or no knowledge of Latin … one could not be asked to follow sermons in an unknown language.'[25]

The fall of Acre in 1291 and the end of military protection for pilgrims meant that alternative provision was required. In 1291, Pope Nicholas IV gained the permission of the Mamluk ruler, Sultan Khalil, for a group of Franciscans to serve in the Holy Sepulchre and to care for its pilgrims. Nine years later, at the representation of Robert of Sicily, the Franciscans were given custody of the church on Mount Sion and of chapels in the Church of the Holy Sepulchre and the Church of the Nativity.

Relations between the Franciscans and the Muslim rulers were often troubled, however, and in 1365 when the Hospitallers besieged Alexandria the friars in Jerusalem were imprisoned. On other occasions the misplaced zeal of the Franciscans led them to court martyrdom by seeking public debate with Muslim authorities and taking the opportunity to insult the prophet Muhammad. Despite such tension however, the pilgrimages resumed, and the Franciscans revived and expanded the sacred topography of Jerusalem and the Holy Land for the benefit of pilgrims. Since preaching was a special charism of the mendicant orders it is reasonable to suppose that preaching must have been an important accompaniment of pilgrim itineraries.

The risks involved in pilgrimage during the later part of the Middle Ages led some pilgrims coming to find substitute 'Holy Lands' nearer to the pilgrims' homes. The remarkable thing is that so many pilgrims did continue to come to the Holy Land. Geoffrey Chaucer (1343-1400) tells us that his

---

[24] *Ibid.*, 177.
[25] *Ibid.*, 190.

fictional Wife of Bath had been to Jerusalem three times.[26] Some real pilgrims were less brave. In 1403 the will of John de Copildik provides one example among many of someone leaving money to send a hired man on pilgrimage to the Holy Land after his death 'for his soul and the forgiveness of his sins.'[27] Queen Isabella, who was a frequent pilgrim to Walsingham ('England's Nazareth'), intended to go to the Holy Sepulchre but chose to ask for dispensation from her vow.[28] For other pilgrims, as with the Wife of Bath, the local pilgrimage centres represented pious additions rather than alternatives to the Holy Land pilgrimage. Thus John de Holderness in Essex, 'while in grave danger on the sea while returning from the Holy Sepulchre vowed to visit in pilgrimage 'all the shrines in the king's realm.'[29]

For those who did get to the Holy Land, the Franciscans were there to cater for their needs by providing hospices and by caring for existing shrines and 'discovering' new ones and by maintaining liturgical functions at these sites. In the 15th century, for example, the friars set up and thus made possible preaching of 'The Stations of the Cross' on the route supposedly taken by Jesus on the way to Calvary. Returning pilgrims helped to keep the Holy Land in the pious imagination of those that preached and prayed back at home. Relics, palms, and other souvenirs from the Holy Land became an important feature of popular devotion. In 1563 Jan van Paesschen, the Carmelite prior at Malines, published a meditative account of a year-long pilgrimage to the Holy Land enabling the devout reader to go to the Holy Land in his or her imagination. This included local 'Stations of the Cross'[30] which were increasingly set up and preached in shrines and eventually in parish churches everywhere.[31]

Meanwhile alongside, and frequently in competition for control of the holy places, Catholic and Orthodox pilgrims continued to come to the Holy Land itself. Among the Orthodox pilgrims, Russian pilgrims revived and extended their own characteristic liturgical institutions in the Holy Land. Helped by improved transport and encouraged by the Russian state, Orthodox

---

[26] Geoffrey Chaucer, 'Prologue to the Canterbury Tale,' lines 464-5.

[27] D Webb, *Pilgrimage in Medieval England*, Hambledon and London, London and New York, 2000, 197.

[28] *Calendars of Entries in the Papal Registers Relating to Great Britain and Ireland*. 3.496 (editor's name not given).

[29] Webb, *op. cit.*, 202.

[30] The term 'Stations' is first used by an English pilgrim, William Wey, who visited Jerusalem in 1468. M Walsh, *A Dictionary of Devotions,* Burns Oates, London, 1993, 251.

[31] In 1731, Pope Clement XII was to extend the indulgences available for those who went on pilgrimage to the Holy Land to all those who devoutly followed the Stations.

pilgrimage reached its height by the end of the 19th century.[32] Most important among the features of Orthodox pilgrimage was attendance at the Holy Week and Easter Liturgies in Jerusalem. In addition, there was the ritual bathing in the river Jordan. This included many of the ceremonies associated with baptism, including the reception of a white garment subsequently laid on the 'Stone of Anointing' in the Church of the Holy Sepulchre and taken home, to serve eventually as the pilgrim's shroud.

For these Russian pilgrims the spiritual and liturgical elements of pilgrimage would have been paramount. Such preaching as might have been included would probably have been little more than exposition of the rituals. Certainly, the historical dimension was a matter of complete irrelevance.[33]

By contrast, 19th century English Protestant pilgrimages were concerned with little apart from the historical. With biblical certainties under fire from historical criticism and the rising tide of historical rationalism, concern with the possibility that archaeology might confirm the truth of Scripture produced a new form of pilgrimage as lecture tour. For the less academically inclined it could be experienced as a devotional evocation of the life and times of Jesus. Travelling in the cultural bubble provided by the Thomas Cook travel agency, the English pilgrims were totally isolated from contact with the local populace or from the strange practices of Orthodox or Catholic Christians.

As with the Russian pilgrimages, these English pilgrimages were fuelled by improvements in communications and by the scramble for influence in this crucial corner of the crumbling Ottoman empire. French ambitions in this regard led to the revival of the Latin Patriarchate and to an increase in Roman Catholic pilgrimages. In due course these acquired some of the qualities of the English Protestant pilgrimages with the significant difference that for the Catholic pilgrims Mass and a devotional homily at the holy places were an essential element in the experience. To this end the Church authorised appropriate readings for use at the altars provided at every shrine

---

[32] 'Throughout history the Russian peasants had travelled to Jerusalem, usually walking the whole way. What changed in the nineteenth century was the development of 'cheap' mass transport and a government policy to encourage pilgrimage.' R Hummel and T Hummel, *Patterns of the Sacred. English Protestant and Russian Orthodox Pilgrims of the Nineteenth Century*, Scorpion Cavendish, London, 1995, 43.

[33] 'The Russian pilgrims expected the Holy Land to be like the Jerusalem pictured in the divine liturgy and in their icons.' '… the Life Giving Tomb is not a mere geographical spot but a place of cosmic significance. The world of divine reality broke in at this spot and the structure of reality—its ontological nature—was altered forever.' *Ibid.*, 52 and 53.

in the care of the Franciscan *Custos*. To the extent that the Mass and the readings commemorated the event associated with the site the homilies preached could be expected to resonate with the readings more often than they would have done at home, particularly before the liturgical reforms of Vatican II.

Clearly, celebration of the Eucharist and other liturgies at the holy sites offer considerable opportunities for more liturgically grounded preaching and the concern with history and geography, 'the world behind the text,' that can inform the pilgrims' understanding of the Gospel message. However, such material alone cannot dictate the direction of the preaching. One or more hermeneutical perspective need to be selected that will take account of 'the world in front of the text.' This world includes the religious, social, and political realities of the Holy Land itself. However, 'the world in front of the text' in Ottoman Palestine was a Muslim culture with indigenous Christian minorities whose experience was very remote from that of Western or Russian pilgrims. As we have seen, foreign pilgrims and native Christians have had less and less to do with each other from the time of the Crusades onwards.

Long before the Crusaders, the developing divisions in the Church had already distanced visiting pilgrims from the indigenous Christian communities. Under Crusader rule, the liturgical celebrations of the large numbers of new pilgrims were of the alien Latin rite that the Crusader kings tried to impose upon the local Church. This process continued after the fall of the Latin Kingdom of Jerusalem when those Western pilgrims intrepid enough to continue coming to the Holy Land would find little in common with the indigenous 'Greek' Orthodox or non-Chalcedonian Christians. Russian pilgrims shared common religious traditions with Orthodox Palestinians, but their language and culture marked them out as strangers. Even more remote were the 19th century Protestant pilgrims from England whose interest in the historical excluded any contact with or interest in the peoples living there in their own times.

Pilgrims from Europe or North America today may have contact with their Catholic or Protestant co-religionists, but most do not. Like the two disciples on the walk to Emmaus, today's pilgrims may not immediately recognise the identity of the person they meet on their journey. It was from the Church of the Holy Land that the West first received the Faith. The pilgrim may discover that the Christians of the Holy Land are now in danger of eventually disappearing from the land of Jesus. As they become aware of the sufferings of the Palestinian people, their sense of gloom invites the questioning of this stranger.

Preaching Plan: Luke 24: 13-25,[34] The Walk to Emmaus
Preparation of the Homily: Process and Strategies

This text narrates the story of the walk to Emmaus and is thus a suitable text to link with a chapter on the history of pilgrimage to the Holy Land. The Lectionary prescribes it for the evening of Easter Day, for Easter Wednesday, and for the Third Sunday of Easter in year A.[35] Competing Holy Land traditions provide three locations for the event. The Byzantines identified the site at Latrun, marked today by a Cistercian abbey. This tradition was unknown to the Crusaders who measured out the Sabbath journey of eleven and a half kilometres and arrived at the nearby village of Abu Ghosh, formerly Qaryat al-Anab (Hebrew: Qiriat Yearim). Here they built the beautiful Church

---

[34] Luke 24: 13-35: Two of the disciples of Jesus were on their way to a village called Emmaus, seven miles from Jerusalem, and they were talking together about all that had happened. Now as they talked this over, Jesus himself came up and walked by their side; but something prevented them from recognising him. He said to them, 'What matters are you discussing as you walk along?' They stopped short, their faces downcast.

Then one of them, called Cleopas, answered him, 'You must be the only person staying in Jerusalem who does not know the things that have been happening there these last few days.' 'What things?' he asked. 'All about Jesus of Nazareth' they answered 'who proved he was a great prophet by the things he said and did in the sight of God and of the whole people; and how our chief priests and our leaders handed him over to be sentenced to death, and had him crucified. Our own hope had been that he would be the one to set Israel free. And this is not all: two whole days have gone by since it all happened; and some women from our group have astounded us: they went to the tomb in the early morning, and when they did not find the body, they came back to tell us they had seen a vision of angels who declared he was alive. Some of our friends went to the tomb and found everything exactly as the women had reported, but of him they saw nothing.'

Then he said to them, 'You foolish men! So slow to believe the full message of the prophets! Was it not ordained that the Christ should suffer and so enter into his glory?' Then, starting with Moses and going through all the prophets, he explained to them the passages throughout the scriptures that were about himself.

When they drew near to the village to which they were going, he made as if to go on; but they pressed him to stay with them. 'It is nearly evening' they said 'and the day is almost over.' So he went in to stay with them. Now while he was with them at table, he took the bread and said the blessing; then he broke it and handed it to them. And their eyes were opened and they recognised him; but he had vanished from their sight. Then they said to each other, 'Did not our hearts burn within us as he talked to us on the road and explained the scriptures to us?'

They set out that instant and returned to Jerusalem. There they found the Eleven assembled together with their companions, who said to them, 'Yes, it is true. The Lord has risen and has appeared to Simon.' Then they told their story of what had happened on the road and how they had recognised him at the breaking of bread.

[35] Acts 2: 14, 22-33 and I Peter 1: 17-21 are the other texts for the third Sunday of Easter. Reference to the Acts passage is used here to illuminate the Gospel passage.

of Notre Dame de l'Arche d'Alliance over a 5th-century church marking the resting place of the Ark as recorded in 1 Samuel 6:21-7:2. Later, after the defeat of the Crusaders at the Horns of Hattin, the route to Jerusalem was changed and a Church at Qubeiba near Ramallah marked a rival Emmaus.[36]

While I have been moved by the experience of visits to all three of these rival shrines, the church and grounds of the abbey at Latrun probably provide the richest autobiographical and narrative preaching resource. Most of the visits to Latrun have been with groups returning to Tel Aviv airport at the conclusion of a pilgrimage, and the thoughts of the pilgrim groups have been full of the impressions received during the itinerary. Like the two disciples, their hearts have been downcast at the Gethsemane and Calvary encountered in recent days—although, like the disciples, their hearts have been warmed by the exposition of the Scriptures and the recognition of their Lord in the Breaking of Bread.

Familiarity with the Gospel text and the experience of preaching on it a number of times—not least at Latrun, as well as the other two pilgrimage sites, has meant that the available commentary texts served only as a secondary resource for preparing this homily.[37] However, there was a useful lesson for the preacher in Luke. This is earmarked by Timothy Johnson's observation that 'in a remarkably down to earth fashion, Luke shows us, narratively, the process by which the first believers actually did learn to understand the significance of the events they had witnessed, and to resolve the cognitive distinction between their experience and their convictions.'[38]

So too, the wisdom of Paul Scott Wilson, that 'the resurrected Jesus may appear to us revealed in strangers, particularly where crucifixion continues today, and in all who are in need and suffering,'[39] helped to crystallise my own thoughts. However, I felt that this sentiment needed anchoring concretely in the sufferings of specific people. The newspapers and television news had recently given wide coverage to a particularly devastating suicide bombing following upon the heels of brutal and murderous incursions into West Bank towns by Israeli forces, and this made it easy for me to focus on sufferings of innocent victims of the Israeli-Palestinian conflict.

---

[36] J Murphy O'Connor, *The Holy Land: An Archaeological Guide From the Earliest Times to 1700*, Oxford University Press, Oxford, 1986, 133-4.

[37] The preaching outlined here is largely based upon a homily preached at three masses for the third Sunday of Easter on the 13-14 April 2002 at Saint Francis de Sales, Hampton Hill.

[38] L T Johnson, *The Gospel of Luke*, Liturgical Press, Collegeville, Minnesota, 1991, 399.

[39] P Wilson, 'Third Sunday of Easter, Year A', E Harn, ed., *The Lectionary Commentary. The Third Readings: The Gospels*, Continuum, New York and London, 2001, 464.

My first homiletic plan began with a life-centred introduction using amusing anecdotes of mistaken identity to illustrate problems of recognition. This was followed by a problematic move on the way in which the preacher and the congregation were, like the two men in the Gospel, downcast, trying in vain to understand the cruel paradoxes of life. The good news move emphasised that the risen Jesus is with his disciples on their journey and is listening to their problems. Afterwards, they realise who the stranger is. Like Peter's audience in Acts, they realise that Jesus was among them, performing miracles of healing and sharing in the sufferings of the poor and the oppressed. The third move seeks to establish an application to liturgy and life. The two disciples recognised Jesus in the breaking of bread, and Christians today can recognise Jesus in the Liturgy of the Word and in the Breaking of Bread. These 'real presences' of the risen Jesus in word and sacrament help us to recognise his real presence in the stranger on our journey. The need to offer shelter and food to the stranger has radical political implications for our unequal world—not least for the Palestinians.

Craddock's *As One Without Authority* was a major influence on the second and final revisions of the homily text to make it more specifically inductive in approach.[40] Craddock advocates a preparatory process as follows: an examination of the 'conception of the sermon,' 'playing with the idea,' 'arriving at clarity,' and finally establishing a 'method of sharing' the insight gained. The amended content focused upon the idea that Christians can recognise Jesus in the Liturgy of the Word and can then recognise him in the Breaking of Bread. These 'real presences' of the risen Jesus in word and sacrament then lead to recognition of his real presence in the stranger on our journey.

Playing with the idea involved a focus upon the notion that some people are insensitive to the presence of the risen Christ in the Eucharist and that this presence seems to them to be unrelated to 'real life.' In addition, many who do believe notionally in the Real Presence find that their 'religious imagination' fails to make connections with their secular experience. An inductive approach to preaching this text will invite the congregation to identify with the two disciples in the Gospel by asking why members of the congregation might be downcast that Sunday. Since it would be easy to settle for a purely personal and subjective 'where-am-I-on-my-faith-journey?' approach, the primary reference point related to the continuing bad news

---

[40] F B Craddock. *As One Without Authority,* rev. ed., Chalice Press, St Louis, Missouri, 2001, 127-9.

about the Israeli–Palestinian conflict. Personal reasons for sadness reinforced the case.

'Arriving at clarity' pointed to the Good News that the risen Christ is with us on our journey and is listening to the tale of human tragedy. Afterwards, as we encounter the risen Christ in the Eucharist, we realise who the stranger was. Like Peter's audience in Acts, we realise that he was among us, performing miracles of healing and sharing in the sufferings of the poor and the oppressed.

The 'method of sharing' involved the recognition that for many people the experience of the Eucharist is an experience of tedium, without any direct connection to everyday interests or concerns. Others have a vivid imaginative apprehension of Christ miraculously present under the outward forms of bread and wine, but they see no relevance in the preaching and proclamation of the Word. An imaginative appeal to narrative addresses both categories of listeners. Both categories need to discover for themselves that recognising Jesus in the Breaking of Bread is strengthened by an intelligent engagement with Christ present in the reading and preaching of the Word. Both modes of presence relate directly to recognition of his presence in the world and in human lives. 'Did not our hearts burn within us as he talked to us on the road.' The detailed application of Easter hope to the tragedies in the newsreel or to personal sadness is left to each listener to determine. On the last occasion on which I preached this homily, the unfolding tragedy in Palestine was competing for space in the news headlines with the funeral of the Queen Mother and the damage sustained by the celebrity footballer, David Beckham, and what this might do for the prospects of the England team!

The Text of the Homily

PROBLEMATIC

It is not hard to identify with the two disciples in the story. A stranger came up and asked, 'What matters are you discussing as you walk along?' And they stopped short, their faces downcast. 'What is the matter with you? You look really miserable.' Everybody in this church must have been asked this question many times in his or her life. Sometimes it may be some matter of public knowledge bugging us. The football star David Beckham's foot injury, perhaps, or maybe something even more serious.

'You must be the only person staying in Jerusalem that does not know the things that have happened these last few days.'

There have been a number of occasions when I have stopped to pray at the Cistercian abbey at Latrun, a quiet and a beautiful place that many believe to have been the original Emmaus. Each time I and the people with me have felt downcast at the sufferings of some of the people we have met on our pilgrimage: people who have lost their homes or their loved ones, people who have no real hope of work or dignity. If I had been staying in Jerusalem these last few days I would have looked and sounded pretty glum. Indeed, I didn't go, but I still feel downcast. My heart goes out to the Israelis killed or maimed by suicide bombs. My heart goes out to the Palestinians killed or maimed in the attack that followed—all the people in need of medical attention that the soldiers did not allow the ambulances to fetch to the hospital. I have many friends in the West Bank cities that have been attacked, and I cannot be certain that they are all alive or unharmed. The news that the Palestinian Christians in Bethlehem were last week prevented from attending Easter Mass for the first time in sixteen hundred years and that the Church of the Nativity was damaged symbolises an absence of Easter joy and a challenge to Easter hope. Even at Latrun in this beautiful and peaceful place associated with the joy of an encounter with the risen Christ there are reminders of sorrow. Just a short distance from the abbey are the ruins of three villages destroyed by the Israelis in 1967.[41] *'What matters are you discussing as you walk along? ... They stopped short, their faces downcast.'*

It is not just the tragedy of what has happened in the Holy Land, but the disappointment of hope. Our hope had been that the peace process in Israel-Palestine would have been going forward like the Northern Ireland peace process that it helped to inspire. It was like that for the two disciples: 'Our hope had been that he would be the one to set Israel free ...'—free from the military occupation of the Romans.

Private disappointments may have touched us too closely to be greatly affected by what is happening in the Holy Land. 'My hope had been that my loved one would have lived a little longer.' 'My hope had been that I would have got the job... found that relationship... recovered fully from that illness ... been able to afford that holiday.' No wonder our faces are downcast. 'Some women from our group have astounded us ...' The two disciples said this as though they did not believe it. We know that faith should make a difference to both private and public disappointment, but we fail to make the connection between the empty tomb and any kind of Good News. The disciples welcomed the stranger but did not see clearly who he was. St Augustine says, 'They walked not with their eyes shut, but there was something within them which did not permit them to know that which they saw.'[42] *How often our faith is like that. We see, but we don't see. We need to be reminded just as the two disciples needed to be reminded on the evening of that first Easter Day: 'You foolish men (and women) so slow to believe the full message of the prophets ....'*

---

[41] 'Imwas, Yalu, and Bayt Nuba—all destroyed by the Israeli defence forces in June 1967 after the area was conquered in the six day war. Many of the inhabitants today live in Ramallah. M Prior, *Zionism and the State of Israel. A Moral Inquiry,* Routledge, London, 1999, 31.

[42] J H Newman, *op. cit.,* 779.

GOOD NEWS

And then there comes recognition. And then we welcome the stranger and invite him to stay, and he takes the bread and gives thanks and breaks it. Then we understand that he was with us all the time. Just like Peter's audience in Acts, we realise that he was among us, performing miracles of healing and sharing in the sufferings of the poor and the oppressed. And then we see him no more, but we remember his words. 'Did not our hearts burn within us as he talked to us on the road and explained the scriptures to us?' And our experience of the risen Christ is confirmed by the experience of others: 'Yes, it is true,' they tell us. 'The Lord has risen and has appeared to Simon.' And we tell our story of what happened on the road and how we recognised him at the breaking of bread.

APPLICATION

Note that everything is seen clearly from the moment that Jesus is recognised as present in the breaking of the bread. It is then that the two disciples realise who it was who had been with them on the road, who it was that had warmed their hearts with his words and whom they had invited into their house. And there is a lesson here for us. The Real Presence of the risen Christ in the Mass is not something isolated from life, it is the prism through which we can see everything else. It is the point at which the tragedies and disappointments of our lives and times can be re-interpreted: 'Did not our hearts burn within us as he talked to us on the road and explained the scriptures to us?' It is also the prism through which we see that the presence in the breaking of bread is not the only real presence. He is present in the Word as it is proclaimed, preached and explained. He is present in the stranger on the road, and, by extension, he is present in the whole human family, especially in the family of believers that we call the Body of Christ and the family of our brothers and sisters in need.

At Mass we can Jesus in the Liturgy of the Word, and then recognise him in the Breaking of Bread. These 'real presences' of the risen Jesus in word and sacrament help us to recognise his real presence in the stranger on our journey. The need to offer shelter and food to the stranger has radical political implications for our unequal world. If the hope and the joy of Easter seem to be very far away from the ugliness of events and from the sadness in our lives we need to recover a way of seeing that centres upon our sharing in the Eucharist. For some that may seem to be an unreal wish. The experience of the Eucharist seems dulled by repetition, and we do not find it easy to make the connection with life. We will recognise Jesus more clearly in the Breaking of Bread if we realise that he is present in the reading and preaching of the Word, preparing to meet us in the Eucharist. And we will recognise Jesus more clearly in the Breaking of Bread if we realise that we are there to celebrate his presence in our world and in our lives. 'Did not our hearts burn within us as he talked to us on the road?' And when we have recognised him we will rush to tell others, 'Yes it is true! The Lord has risen!'

Chapter 3
THE WORLD OF THE HOLY LAND:
BEHIND THE TEXT AND
IN FRONT OF THE TEXT

*And you shall be my witnesses in Jerusalem in all Judea and Samaria
and to the end of the earth (Acts 1: 8) [RSV].*

Sometimes these elements can provide avenues towards understanding
analogous realities in the Holy Land today. Significantly, however, they can
also illuminate Christian theological understanding of the world beyond the
Holy Land, The world of the Holy Land is the world of the Gospels. Whenever
and wherever the Gospel is preached, understanding of that world is an
essential part of the background to the text. As we have seen in the first two
chapters, the desire to experience that world and to investigate its history
provided one of the motives over the centuries for coming on pilgrimage to
the Holy Land. Certainly the Holy Land can provide rich insights into that
'world behind the text'. The geography and archaeology of Israel-Palestine
can illuminate the historical background of the Gospel texts. This world
includes historical, religious, political, and cultural elements that are often
complex and unfamiliar to the modern reader or to the pilgrims who go to
the Holy Land today. Sometimes these elements can provide avenues towards
understanding analogous realities in the Holy Land today. Significantly, however,
they can also illuminate the preaching context of the world beyond the
Holy Land, what is represented in the Acts of the Apostles as the 'the uttermost
parts of the earth' (Acts 1: 8).

The preacher with personal experience of the Holy Land can
appreciate the opportunities available for preaching provided by the
historical and geographical context of the Gospel narrative. The richness
of background geographical and archaeological material for biblical study
is also of great potential value to the preacher. Preachers everywhere, like
pilgrimage leaders and teachers of biblical studies, must sometimes engage
the task of addressing questions of historicity. The relationship between
Jesus Christ and the Gospels should be seen both in terms of a testimony
to faith and as witness to historical event. An approach that does justice to
both these two imperatives will steer between the unacceptable extremes
of biblical literalism and an unexamined prejudice that invariably excludes
the possibility that the scriptural record may sometimes refer to a real
event. Thus, although a preacher may be primarily concerned with the

difference a text can make to the lives of his listeners, he is always confronted with the secondary issue of what 'actually happened'.

In addressing this issue, geographical criteria should be seen as fulfilling a function analogous to the apparatus of textual criticism in the development of the preacher's understanding of the historical realities behind a text. Gospels in modern scholarship are seen, not as biography as understood in the world of today, but as containing biographical material refracted through the 'paschal imagination' of the early Church. Sandra Schneiders offers a particularly valuable insight on the question of historicity in relation to the question of the historical Jesus.[1] For Schneiders, the historical Jesus is the actual Jesus after he has been mediated through the faith-concerns and imagination of the Gospel writers and of those who passed on the earlier unwritten traditions about Jesus.[2]

The physical geography of the Holy Land can contribute to our understanding of both the actual Jesus and of the historical Jesus.[3] Sometimes it will indicate a surprising closeness between the actual Jesus and the historical Jesus of the text. For example, there are several instances in the Fourth Gospel where physical geography suggests that the Jesus of the narrative may be nearer to the actual Jesus than was previously supposed,[4] or at least

---

[1] Schneiders distinguishes between the *actual Jesus* (or the *real Jesus*) and the *historical Jesus*. Both of these are distinct from the *proclaimed Jesus*. The relationship between the actual, the historical and the proclaimed Jesus is seen as complementary. Thus; 'The gospels' Jesus (the proclaimed Jesus of the text or the 'textual Jesus' ...) is more than the historical Jesus insofar as the gospels present not only history but the transhistorical, not only facts but theological interpretation of facts.' S M Schneiders, *The Revelatory Text: Interpreting the New Testament as Sacred Scripture*, Liturgical Press, Collegeville, Minnesota, 1999, 108-9.

[2] 'The historical Jesus, as the medium of the proclaimed Jesus, is the taproot of the authentic faith in the real Jesus and the norm of the Church's proclamation.' S M Schneiders, *ibid.*, 110.

[3] Although topographical references are largely ignored in the Form Critical approach to the Gospels, Conzelmann, in his *The Theology of Saint Luke,* acknowledges their 'extreme importance for understanding the Gospels in their present redaction—not so much from a historical point of view, but because of the theological vision they serve.' R Collins, *Introduction to the New Testament*, SCM Press, London, 1983, 211.

[4] For example, see the passage describing the dialogue between Jesus and the Samaritan woman in John 4. Although there is no evidence that it was Jacob's Well, there is indeed a well, situated near to the modern Palestinian city of Nablus and the ancient Israelite city of Shechem. This well, at the intersection of two roads, would have been a natural stopping place for Jesus on his journey, and its existence renders the account of his dialogue with the woman in John 4 more plausible as actual event. So, too, with the healing of the man at the pool of Bethesda in John 5: 2-9 and the healing of the blind man at the pool of Siloam in John 9. In each case the circumstantial evidence that the pools existed at the time of Jesus, together with the archaeological data surrounding their use, suggests that the author of the Fourth Gospel places his narrative within the framework of real places.

more than the radically sceptical critics have supposed.[5] In other cases the geographical evidence will indicate that the text is much more remote from the 'real' event. The first preaching plan in the second part of this section has been chosen to illustrate just such a remoteness—a case where the evidence forces the preacher back to a primarily symbolic interpretation of the text.[6]

One of the religious realities in the Holy Land that can lay claim to illuminating the meaning of a text is the faith and practice of observant Jews. These realities may offer some useful reference points for the Christian preacher. However, such references should be made with care. A good case can be made for saying that living Judaism is a product of the Talmud and is, therefore, later than Christianity, even though the term 'Judaism' is often applied loosely to the Judaic religion of the 1st century AD. Rather than talk about 'Judaism' in the 1st century or at any other time, it would be more accurate to speak of several contemporary 'Judaisms'.[7] Whatever term is applied to the religion of that time, however, the 'Judaisms' or proto-Judaisms of the 1st century clearly can provide some otherwise unavailable insights. Likewise, an awareness of modern Judaisms, in the Israeli context, and elsewhere, can sometimes provide illustrative analogies with the religious world of Jesus.[8]

---

[5] For example Rudolf Bultmann, whose scepticism regarding the historicity of the Synoptic Gospels is even greater in respect of John. In his 1941 commentary, *The Gospel of John*, he argued that the Gospel as we have it represents an attempt to produce an orthodox redaction of a semi-Gnostic collection of sayings and narrative material drawn from various sources by a formerly Gnostic convert to mainstream early Christianity. This author and the redactor would both have been unfamiliar with the Holy Land (J Kselman and R Witherup, 'Modern New Testament Criticism,' R Brown *et al.*, eds., *The New Jerome Biblical Commentary*, Geoffrey Chapman, London, 1990, 1138). This unfamiliarity would have been one that was shared by Bultmann—who never set foot in Palestine! Either the author and/or the redactor were better acquainted with the geographical locations than Bultmann supposed, or else he is referring to traditions regarding real events that took place in real places.

[6] For a homiletic preaching based on a passage judged by the present writer to be shown to indicate a greater convergence between text and event, a preaching plan based on John 4 has been included at the conclusion of Chapter V, 'Multi Faith Pluralism in the Holy Land'.

[7] 'The name Judaism emerged at around the opening of the Christian era (2 Maccabees 2: 21, 8: 1, 14: 38; Galatians 1: 13). Like other aggregating names of major religions it is misleading if it implies that there is uniformity of belief and practice among all Jews.' L Cohn-Sherbok, 'Judaism', J Bowker, ed., *The Oxford Dictionary of World Religions*, Oxford University Press, Oxford 1997, 512.

[8] 'Jesus was born of the Jewish people, as were his Apostles and a large number of his first disciples. When he revealed himself as the Messiah and Son of God (cf. Mt. 16: 16), the bearer of the new Gospel message, he did so at the fulfillment and perfection of the earlier Revelation. And, although his teaching had a profoundly new character, Christ nevertheless, in many instances, took his stand on the teaching of the Old Testament. The New Testament is profoundly marked by its relation to the Old.' 'Guidelines on Religious Relations with the Jews,' §4, A Flannery, *Documents of Vatican II*, Dominican Publications, Dublin, 1982, 747.

This said, the Judaism of modern Israel is not only diverse in its spirituality, theology, and politics; it also is uneven in its presence and influence.[9] However, whatever may be learned from Jewish society in modern Israel, the models of social and cultural life in the peasant society in which Jesus lived find more parallels in Palestinian and other Arab societies.[10] Such parallels are certainly stronger than with mainstream modern secular Western societies (including Israel), where most Jews live today.[11]

Thus, preachers who have visited the Holy Land or who have studied accounts of its geography and culture are able to draw on this in their preaching. For example, patterns of farming and of social life have, until very recently, remained largely unchanged over centuries. Watch towers[12] and landmarks[13] survive to offer visual echoes of Old Testament symbols. Palestinian peasants farm olive groves and fig trees much as they did in the time of Jesus, and Palestinian shepherds, then as now, do not drive their sheep as Western shepherds do—they lead them.

There are also a number of parallels between the society in which Jesus lived and peasant society in the Middle East today. One important element in the world of the Gospels still surviving in Arab society is the patron-client relationship by which power, influence, inducement, and commitment are exchanged between persons of unequal social standing.[14] In common with most 20th-century Palestinians, Jesus lived in an extended family that constituted an economic unit[15] in which parents controlled the choice of a marriage partner within a defined social group. The bride lived with the bridegroom's family and her virginity before marriage[16] and faithfulness to her husband after it[17] were both important elements in a code of shame and honour that operated both at the individual and the family or

---

[9] 'It would be a falsification to suggest that Judaism, the religion, is being revived everywhere in Israel.' N Bentwich, in Arberry, *op. cit.*, 10.

[10] Modern Palestinian society is changing dramatically under Western influences. The early stages of this change are described in A Schölch, *Palestine in Transformation, 1856-1882: Studies in Social, Economic and Political Development*, Institute for Palestine Studies, Washington, DC, 1993.

[11] For a summary of the main differences between family in the United States (the country with the largest number of Jews) and first century Palestine, see K C Hanson and D E Oakman, *Palestine in the Time of Jesus-Social Structures and Social Conflicts*, Augsburg Press, Minneapolis 1998, 22.

[12] 2 Chronicles 20: 24 and Isaiah 21: 5, 8.

[13] Deut. 19: 14, 27: 17; Proverbs 22: 28, 23: 10; Job 24: 2.

[14] E.g., Luke 16: 1-9.

[15] E.g., Matthew 4: 8-22, 22: 1: 28, Luke 15: 11-32.

[16] E.g., Matthew 1: 18-25.

[17] Luke 16: 18.

clan level. In such a society promiscuity was abhorred, particularly in women,[18] and adultery was, in principle at least, punishable by death.[19] Inheritance rights for sons had relative priority over those of daughters.[20] These laws derived directly from the Pentateuch and are very similar to those embodied in Islamic Shari'ah governing modern practice among Palestinians.[21]

Although, in some respects at least, large sections of rural peasant culture have remained unchanged for centuries, today under the influence of Western modernity and of economic change, traditional values are undergoing enormous change throughout Middle Eastern society. This is particularly the case for those values governing gender and family life.[22]

Preaching in the Holy Land itself takes place in an area both of religious, social, and cultural continuities and change. It also takes place in the context of contested political realities and issues that constantly confront the pilgrim. In the wider context of preaching, there are a range of other realities and issues. Some of the realities and issues are specific to the local situation. Others are of global significance and must contribute to the hermeneutical perspective of the preacher. Likewise, there are some realities and issues that are specific to the Holy Land, but there are others that have importance for everyone. For preachers and congregations outside the Holy Land, the preaching hermeneutic, 'the world in front of the text,' will be concerned with matters of relevance to whichever part of the 'uttermost parts of the earth' provides the context for the preaching. Nevertheless, Israel-Palestine can never be far from the mind of any preacher or congregation, wheresoever situated. This is partly because human beings live increasingly in a 'global village' in which regional issues have planetary-wide significance. For historical and geopolitical reasons the Israeli-Palestinian conflict is just such an issue. In addition, the Holy Land has a special significance for Christians, Jews, and Muslims everywhere. In Christian preaching the biblical text itself constantly refers us back to the land that is proclaimed as being in some special way the arena of God's revelation and saving actions in history.

---

[18] Luke 7: 37-39.

[19] John 8: 3-4.

[20] Mark 12: 7 and parallels, Luke 15: 11.

[21] Christian Palestinians experienced something similar in the administration of family and customary law by Church Courts under the *millet* system during Ottoman times. See A O'Mahony, 'The Religious, Political and Social Status of the Christian Communities in Palestine: c. 1800-1930', A O'Mahony, *et al.*, eds., *The Christian Heritage in the Holy Land*, Scorpion Cavendish, London, 1995. 237-65.

[22] See G Menucci, 'Kulthum Auda, Palestinian Ethnographer: Gendering the Palestinian Landscape', in Abu Lughod, *et al.,* eds., *Landscape of Palestine: Equivocal Poetry*, West Bank Publications, Birzeit University, Birzeit, 1999, 79-94.

The fact that those who take sides in the modern Israeli-Palestinian conflict frequently invoke the Bible makes it even more difficult to ignore what is taking place in the land where it all began.[23]

Those preaching in 'the uttermost parts of the earth' do not have to deal with the unfamiliar context of the Holy Land in quite the same way as those involved in leading pilgrimages there. However they have the same problems of interpreting complex historical, religious, and political issues pertaining to the land that is constantly on their lips while they preach. Moreover challenges and opportunities that are present everywhere may present themselves in a particularly powerful way when related to context of the Holy Land. The preaching plans that follow have been chosen to illustrate this thesis.

Preaching Plan 1: Mark 5: 1-10,[24] The Gerasene Demoniac and the Flight of the Swine

Preparation of the Homily: Process and Strategies

---

[23] Michael Prior offers an account of the use of Scripture to justify oppression in the Holy Land and explores parallels with religious justification of other rapacious colonial enterprises. M Prior, *The Bible and Colonialism*, Sheffield Academic Press, Sheffield, 1997.

[24] Mark 5: 1-10: Jesus and his disciples reached the country of the Gerasenes on the other side of the lake, and no sooner had he left the boat than a man with a unclean spirit came out from the tombs towards him. The man lived in the tombs and no one could secure him any more, even with a chain, because he had often been secured with fetters and chains but had snapped the chains and broken the fetters, and no one had the strength to control him. All night and all day, among the tombs and in the mountains, he would howl and gash himself with stones. Catching sight of Jesus from a distance, he ran up and fell at his feet and shouted at the top of his voice, 'What do you want from me, Jesus, son of the Most high God? Swear by God you will not torture me!' – For Jesus had been saying to him, 'Come out of the man, unclean spirit.' What is your name?' Jesus asked. 'My name is legion,' he answered 'for there are many of us.' And he begged him earnestly not to send them out of the district. Now there was there on the mountainside a great herd of pigs feeding and the unclean spirit begged him, 'Send us to the pigs, let us go into them. So he gave them leave. With that, the unclean spirits came out and went into the pigs, and the herd of about two thousand pigs charged down the cliff into the lake, and there they were drowned. The swineherds ran off and told their story in the town and in the country round about; and the people came to see what really happened. They came to Jesus and saw the demoniac sitting there, clothed and in his full senses – the very man who had had the legion in him before – and they were afraid. And those who had witnessed it reported what had happened to the demoniac and what had become of the pigs. Then they began to implore Jesus to leave the neighbourhood. As he was getting into the boat, the man who had been possessed begged to be allowed to stay with him. Jesus would not let him but said to him, 'Go home to your people and tell them all that the Lord in his mercy has done for you .' So the man went off and proceeded to spread throughout the Decapolis all that Jesus had done for him. And everyone was amazed.

It is perhaps not surprising that this passage is not included in the three-year Sunday Cycle.[25] It is a text that reveals a remoteness between story and event and the evidence of geography confirms that remoteness.[26] The preaching outline included here takes the geographical and historical critical ambiguity as one of the starting points of the homily, linking it with my own personal experience of the demonic as revealed in Israel-Palestine in our own day.

My first experiences of visiting the Byzantine Church at Kursi[27] were coloured by vivid and sometimes traumatic impressions of present political realities, of deprivation and oppression, violence and counter-violence. Preaching to pilgrims at the site and preaching on this text subsequently has always been a struggle between the immediacy of present conflicts in the Holy Land and the fabulous character of the Gospel passage. The many faceted character of the power of evil provides the link: 'My name is Legion ... for there are many of us.' This problematic introduction leads on into the central proclamation of the Good News and a focus upon the amazing power of Jesus to overcome evil in all its pervasive destructiveness. The application of this message then reaffirms faith in this power of Christ and applies it to communal and individual situations that exist in the worlds of the hearers, 'the world in front of the text.'

---

[25] It does figure, however, in the weekday readings and is appointed to be read on the Monday of the Fourth Week in Ordinary Time.

[26] The confusion over the location, together with absence of 'a steep bank' for the pigs to rush down from into the sea, combine with other intrinsically unlikely elements in the story to reinforce scepticism about what actually happened. The conclusion suggested seems to show that the exorcism was part of the ministry of the 'actual Jesus' but that the story about the swine is 'an added satire mocking the Romans' reflecting events of around 66 AD. According to Rousseau and Arav, this is 'a date that fits with the date generally accepted for the final redaction of Mark.' (J Rousseau and R Arav, *Jesus and His World. An Archaeological and Cultural Dictionary*, Fortress Press, Minneapolis, 1995, 98). The date for the final redaction of Mark is a matter of controversy among scholars but is usually between 65 and 75 AD (M Hooker, *The Gospel of Mark*, A and C Black, London, 1991, 8). A minority of scholars, notably J A T Robinson, in his *Dating of the New Testament,* place the date of Mark earlier than this, but any date between 66 and 76 would fit the hypothesis of a simple exorcism, embroidered in the retelling with a satirical addition about a Roman 'Pig Legion' being driven into the sea.

[27] In Matthew 5: 1, the exorcism is seen as taking place 'in the district of the Gerasenes' (in some manuscripts 'Gadarenes', as in Matthew's Gospel). Gadara is usually identified with Umm Qais some thirty miles away from the Sea of Galilee, four miles north of the river Yarmuk and seven miles east of the Jordan. The geographical location of the territory of the Gaderenes stretched to the area east of the southern part of the Sea of Galilee. However, the episode is traditionally commemorated by the Byzantine church and monastery at Kursi on the north east of the Sea of Galilee, where there also are the remains of an earlier shrine. J Murphy O'Connor, *The Holy Land: An Archaeological Guide From Earliest Times to 1700,* Oxford University Press, Oxford, 1986, 263.

Outline Text of Homily

PROBLEMATIC

I have two problems about this text. First of all the details sound a bit improbable, and secondly they are more than a little frightening. I have had the opportunity to visit the place where it is believed that this event took place. There is no cliff, and the pigs would have needed to fly horizontally for several hundred yards before they could have fallen headlong into the sea! Maybe that does not matter too much. Perhaps it was a different place. But a man is possessed by devils, and Jesus casts them out and sends them into a herd of pigs! Most of us no longer think of evil as working in quite that way. However, if we use our imagination we can feel quite scared by the sense of the power of the demonic that the story communicates to us. And the demonic is still with us 'My name is Legion because there are many of us.'

When my journey brought me to the traditional site of this episode, I came with a very strong sense of the demonic. It was not the demonic that possesses pigs and drives them into the sea but the demonic that drives people out of their homes and is capable of filling at least some of them with a hunger for revenge that has the power to produce yet more demons. I am talking, of course, about the sufferings of the Palestinians and the violence that that those sufferings sometimes give rise to.

Anyone who has ever been on a pilgrimage to the Holy Land and ventured beyond the hotel and the air-conditioned coach will understand what I am talking about. Evil drives people to madness, and the power of evil is legion: 'My name is Legion because there are many of us.'

GOOD NEWS

Well, the good news is that the man was cured. 'They came to Jesus and saw the demoniac sitting there, clothed and in his full senses.' The political problems of the Holy Land remain. Please God, one day they will be solved. But certainly, the demons will reappear somewhere else. We have only to turn on the TV to see news about the power of the demonic in our world. 'My name is Legion because there are many of us.'

We can find evil much nearer home too, and we can find it in our own hearts. 'My name is legion because there are many of us.' But the good news is that the power of Christ is greater than the power of evil.

APPLICATION TO LITURGY AND LIFE

At this Eucharist we celebrate the power of Christ over evil. We can see—some of us may have experienced ourselves—his healing power to bring us back to our senses, to change our lives for the better. At this Eucharist we celebrate our faith that the power of evil has been and is being overcome. And in this Eucharist we commit ourselves to being like Christ—by casting out demons. And we do this not least by our solidarity with the oppressed—not just the Palestinians but oppressed people everywhere—and by praying and working for a more just world.

Preaching Plan 2: Luke 2: 1-14, Isaiah 9: 1-7, and Titus 2: 11-14,[28]
The Message to the Shepherds

Preparation of the Homily: Process and Strategies

By way of example of the relevance of the Holy Land to preaching, this outline homily represents a synthesis of preaching given during pilgrimages at the Church of the Nativity and in the Shepherds' Field, together with several Christmas homilies preached over a period of ten years. The contents of this preaching plan were not only influenced by the study of the texts and of the world behind those texts but also by the preacher's personal experiences of the Holy Land. The Christmas homilies for 2000 and for 2001

---

[28] Isaiah 9:1-7:

The people that walked in darkness
has seen a great light;
on those who live in a land of deep shadow
a light has shone.
You have made their gladness greater,
you have made their joy increase;
they rejoice in your presence
as men rejoice at harvest time,
as men are happy when they are dividing the spoils.

For the yoke that was weighing on him,
the bar across his shoulders,
the rod of his oppressor,
these you break as on the day of Midian.

For all the footgear of battle,
every cloak rolled in blood,
is burnt,
and consumed by fire.

For there is a child born for us,
a son given to us
and dominion is laid on his shoulders;
and this is the name they give him:
Wonder-Counsellor, Mighty-God,
Eternal-Father, Prince-of-Peace.
Wide is his dominion
in a peace that has no end,
for the throne of David
and for his royal power,
which he establishes and makes secure
in justice and integrity.
From this time onwards and for ever,
the jealous love of the Lord of Hosts will do this.

Titus 2: 11-14: God's grace has been revealed, and it has made salvation possible for the whole human race and taught us that what we have to do is to give up everything that does

were preached in the light of news reports of the devastation caused by the Israeli attacks on Palestinian towns and villages in the Bethlehem area.

The central theme of the homily given here and its subsequent development derived primarily from a sense of amazement and genuine awe inspired by the doctrine of the Incarnation. It also sprang from a personal and political involvement with the ongoing passion of the Palestinian people, not least in the villages of Beit Jala and Beit Sahur and in the refugee camps around Bethlehem.[29]

The preaching plan employs a political liberationist hermeneutic that attempts to relate events in and around Bethlehem to comparable events in the wider world political situation, taking its stand on the social teaching of the Catholic Church. These include its critique of consumer capitalism, support of trades unions and the right to strike, concern for the oppressed, and, more recently, opposition to the effects of globalisation.[30] In my particular

---

not lead to God, and all our worldly ambitions; we must be self-restrained and live good and religious lives here in this present world, while we are waiting in hope for the blessing which will come with the Appearing of the glory of our great God and saviour Christ Jesus. He sacrificed himself for us in order to set us free from all wickedness and to purify a people so that it could be his very own and would have no ambition except to do good.

Luke 2: 1-14: Caesar Augustus issued a decree for a census of the whole world to be taken. This census—the first—took place while Quirinius was governor of Syria, and everyone went to his own town to be registered. So Joseph set out from the town of Nazareth in Galilee and travelled up to Judaea, to the town of David called Bethlehem, since he was of David's House and line, in order to be registered together with Mary, his betrothed, who was with child. While they were there the time came for her to have her child, and she gave birth to a son, her first-born. She wrapped him in swaddling clothes, and laid him in a manger because there was no room for them at the inn. In the countryside close by there were shepherds who lived in the fields and took it in turns to watch their flocks during the night. The angel of the Lord appeared to them and the glory of the Lord shone round them. They were terrified, but the angel said, 'Do not be afraid. Listen, I bring you news of great joy, a joy to be shared by the whole people. Today in the town of David a saviour has been born to you; he is Christ the Lord. And here is a sign for you: you will find a baby wrapped in swaddling clothes and lying in a manger.' And suddenly with the angel there was a great throng of the heavenly host, praising God and singing:

'Glory to God in the highest heaven
and peace to men who enjoy his favour.'

[29] Some of the author's earlier experiences in this area were recorded in 'Letter from Bir Zeit', *Middle East International,* 26 March 1982, and 'Letter from Bethlehem', *Middle East International,* 19 December 1987.

[30] These social teachings can be found in the corpus of papal social teachings ranging from Leo XIII's encyclical *Rerum Novarum* in 1891 to Pius XI's *Quadragesimo Anno* in 1931, John XXIII's *Mater et Magistra* in 1961, Paul VI's *Populorum Progressio* in 1967, and John Paul II's *Centesimus Annus* in 1991.

concern for the rights of the Palestinians, I welcome the consistent advocacy by the Holy See for peace and justice in the Holy Land, making allowances for my own regret that such advocacy has not been more vigorous and prophetic.[31]

I have preached regularly to several different congregations at Christmas time—typically in two largely middle class suburban parishes and at the college chapel where the out-of-term congregation is socially very similar. At Christmas, in particular, worshippers include all degrees of religious commitment and educational background. Members of the congregation might be expected to have an uneven degree of knowledge about the Holy Land in biblical times and a similarly uneven background in their awareness of, or interest in, the contemporary situation.

In my preparatory reading, which focussed primarily upon the Gospel reading, I found an emphasis on the nature of the Davidic Messiah as one bringing about the eschatological gift of peace, as well as a stress on powerlessness of the Christ Child in bringing that about.[32] Extracts from the Church Fathers found in a patristic commentary gave added depth to the insights on the poverty of Christ in his Incarnation. Thus, for example, Bede who is included among the earlier fathers in this volume, refers to God 'confined in the narrow space of a rude manger, whose seat is in the heavens.'[33] On the significance of the shepherds going in haste, Ambrose comments, 'Let this not seem to you a slight example of faith, because of the humble character of the shepherds ... for no one indolently seeks after Christ.'[34] A feminist commentator, Loretta Dornisch, speculates—to little useful purpose— that some of the shepherds might have been women.[35] but emphasises the universal significance of the common binding clothes in which the baby was wrapped. She also offers the useful insight that the call of the shepherds

---

[31] For a comprehensive list of statements up to 1990, see A Kreutz, *Vatican Policy on the Palestinian-Israeli Conflict*, Greenwood, New York, 1990. Documentation on the statements by John Paul II in 1996 can be found in *PASSIA 1996 (Palestinian Academy Society for the Study of International Affairs)*. Speeches made during his visit to the Holy Land in 2000 are available in *PASSIA* 2001 and on the Vatican website. For a critical analysis of the Holy See-Israel Fundamental Agreement of 1993, see M Prior, *Zionism and the State of Israel, A Moral Enquiry*, Routledge, London and New York, 1999, 109-12.

[32] R J Karris, 'The Gospel According to Luke', R E Brown, *et al.*, eds., *The New Jerome Biblical Commentary*, Geoffrey Chapman, London, 1990, 682.

[33] J H Newman, *Catena Aurea. Commentary on the Four Gospels Collected Out of the Works of the Fathers by Saint Thomas Aquinas, Volume Three: Saint Luke*, The Saint Austin Press, Southampton, 1997, (first published in English in 1941), 68.

[34] *Ibid.*, 74.

[35] L Dornisch, *A Woman Reads Luke*, Liturgical Press, Collegeville, Minnesota, 1999, 30.

to the manger has wider significance: 'The shepherds decide to go and see the sign that the Lord has made known to them. The implied reader who is called to faith and discipleship through the same good news is called to the same kind of decision.'[36]

Reference to a social science commentary provided an emphasis on the details of the shepherds as a despised and humble social group.[37] Another commentary made points that converged with and assisted my own homiletic theme by including an emphasis upon the fear of the shepherds being replaced by joy,[38] and their response to the angels' message as 'the prototype of the community of faith.'[39] On the other hand, in the light of the current situation in the Holy Land, I found the same commentary offered an over-ready spiritualisation of the peace of Christmas.[40]

Catherine Hilkert makes a distinction between the use of a dialectical and a sacramental imagination in preaching.[41] Dialectical imagination challenges the congregation with the power of God's word, calling to judgement and repentance, and sacramental imagination invites the hearers to recognise the affirming presence of Christ in their lives. This homily attempts to do both. The good news is both affirming and challenging. The peace of Christ has come: '*He is present—not just in the sacraments—but in our families, in our homes, at our workplace or school, in our friendships.*' But the peace of Christ should be a real peace and should be allowed to challenge the injustices of Palestine or of the world—just as much as it should challenge the injustice in the hearts of those who hear it proclaimed: '*It will not be a manageable joy. It is a joy that will not leave us comfortable. It will 'knock us off our perch!*'

Text of Homily
PROBLEMATIC

I want you to imagine that you are suddenly called out of your work place or your school to receive an urgent message. Since the message is an urgent one, it is obviously going to be something to make you happy or something to make you sad. Maybe you will be happy because you have won the lottery! Perhaps it is news of bereavement or the

[36] *Ibid.*, 31.

[37] B Malina, and R Rohrbraugh, *Social-Science Commentary on the Synoptic Gospels*, Fortress Press, Minneapolis, 1992, 296.

[38] K F Nickle, *Preaching the Gospel of Luke: Proclaiming God's Rule*, Westminster Knox, Louisville, Kentucky, 2000, 24.

[39] *Ibid.*, 25.

[40] *Ibid.*, 265.

[41] M C Hilkert, *Naming Grace: Preaching and the Sacramental Imagination*, Continuum, New York, 1997, 19-43.

news that you need an operation. In that case you are going to be sad or, maybe, frightened. Because the message is such an urgent one, it will not be anything trivial. It will either be something to reassure you or to challenge you to conversion, prayer, and action. Tonight's message is both. It is not simply a comfortable piece of news. 'The shepherds were terrified.' They were also reassured when they were told: 'Do not be afraid; for see—I am bringing you good news of great joy for all the people.'

The message of Christmas is that God is with us (Emmanuel). God is present with us in our world—not in a 'winter wonderland'—not in a tinsel-covered fantasyland—but in our world. This is joyful news. He is present—not just in the sacraments—but in our families, in our homes, at our workplace or school, in our friendships. God is present in Jesus—in our world. There is no need to be afraid. Peace has been declared: 'Glory to God in the highest heaven, and on earth peace among those who are God's friends.'

That might be a good point to end. Everyone could be happy. But it can't, because it doesn't quite ring true. Families can be problematic as well as joyful. Homes can be repossessed. Work can be unrewarding—even for the people who can find jobs. Friendships can be broken. And as for peace! There are dozens of wars going on at this moment that the TV and the papers don't even bother to mention any more. More people have died in the little wars since the end of the Second World War than died in the Second World War itself.

What about the birthplace of Jesus? The second time that I ever visited Bethlehem in 1982 I was taken to meet a family whose house was right by the Shepherds' Field. I say 'was' because the house had just been destroyed by the Israeli military. Two of the boys in the family had been accused of throwing stones at an Israeli military vehicle. The boys had been arrested and held without trial, and the house had been flattened. The mother, who was very pregnant, and her young daughter were making the best of it on a plastic settee in a tent while the father of the family was trying to rebuild his house. That was a powerful and terrible moment for me, as well as for all the other people who were with us. A little later the group celebrated Mass in the Church of the Nativity nearby. In our minds we all made the connection between the Holy Family of Jesus, Mary, and Joseph and the poor Palestinian family whose plight we had just seen.

Since then other events at the 'little town of Bethlehem' have spoiled the Christmas story for us. Today, as in the Gospel passage I have just read, shepherds would be right to be afraid—they are in the line of fire! Around Christmas 2001, hundreds of Bethlehem people have been shot—mainly Palestinian children, including Palestinian Christians. There are many parallels between the current situation in Bethlehem and that which the Christmas story presents to us. Then, as now, the town was under military occupation. In Luke's Gospel there was 'no room at the inn.' [42] *In Matthew's*

---

[42] Luke 2: 8.

account of the birth of Christ, the Holy family became a refugee family, and mothers were crying for their children.[43] *Some things in the Gospel accounts have similarities with the reality in Bethlehem today.*

It is good to know that 'a child has been born for us ... a Prince of Peace.'[44] *It is comforting to be told that 'His authority shall grow continually, and there shall be endless peace,'*[45] *but where is the evidence? At first sight it is a joke. We were looking for a great king to put things right, and we see the utterly vulnerable image of a baby in swaddling clothes—the 1st-century equivalent of a nappy. They laid him in a manger, in a food trough for cattle! He was utterly dependent on his mother. Let us not sentimentalise this baby! God in Jesus became vulnerable, shared our darkness and our hurt, all the way from the manger to the grave.*

GOOD NEWS

Why did he do it? Because he loves us so much. His weakness subverts all our false ideas about status and wealth and power. So he will have the victory promised in Isaiah, destroying oppression and war: 'For the yoke of their burden, and the bar across their shoulders the rod of their oppressor, you have broken.'[46] *Why did he do it? To change our values and priorities: 'Jesus sacrificed himself for us in order to set us free from all wickedness.'*[47]

APPLICATION TO LITURGY AND LIFE

Like the Shepherds we need to act—to go in faith to the manger. Then the birth of Christ will give us greater joy than we could ever have imagined. But it will not be a manageable joy. It is a joy that will not leave us comfortable. It will knock us off our perch! If we make that journey of faith to Bethlehem, we will want to show solidarity with the poor Palestinian shepherds and the homeless family. We will also realise that it is not only in Bethlehem that there are poor and homeless people demanding our solidarity. We will find them all over the world. We will find them in our own country. And the strength we will need, if we are we are to be in solidarity with the homeless and the poor, is to be found in the joy that we celebrate at this Eucharist.

---

[43] Matthew 2: 13–18.

[44] Isaiah 9: 6.

[45] Isaiah 9: 7.

[46] Isaiah 9: 3.

[47] Titus 2: 14.

Chapter 4
THE ECUMENICAL PERSPECTIVE
AND THE PREACHING OF THE GOSPEL IN
THE HOLY LAND

The hour is coming, and now is, when those who worship God will worship him in spirit and in truth (John 4: 23a).

Within the perspective of Holy Land studies, the preacher will employ appropriate interpretative approaches that will include an awareness of Christian ecumenical and inter-faith realities. Pilgrims to the Holy Land will identify a rich variety of often competing Christian communities present in the Holy Land today. Sensitivity to this phenomenon requires that the preacher of pilgrimage should include a strongly ecumenical awareness in his or her preaching. Furthermore, not only is Christian pluralism a pre-requisite for preaching within the perspective of Holy Land studies. So, too, is an awareness of a wider pluralism of the three great religions—and, by extension, of all the great world religions. One of the primary religious realities of the Holy Land is that it is holy to the three Abrahamic and Semitic faiths: Christianity, Islam, and Judaism.

Before exploring the challenges and opportunities for pluralistic ecumenical and inter-faith approaches to preaching in relation to the Holy Land, this chapter will offer an account of the diversity of Christian presence in the Holy Land. It also will argue that foreign powers and even foreign pilgrims have either brought about or reinforced rival Christian presences among the indigenous population. More recently, there are a number of signs that understanding and solidarity among this Christian population is growing. This chapter will suggest that a Holy Land perspective can provide preachers and leaders of pilgrimages with opportunities to contribute to assisting this process by building closer bonds between Christians of different traditions both in the Holy Land and world-wide. The chapter will conclude with a preaching plan to illustrate the relevance of the Holy Land perspective for preaching in the wider ecumenical context.

Acting, as the Holy Land does, as a pole of attraction for Christian pilgrims from all over the world, it might be supposed that the Holy Land would be a focus of unity among Christians. Unfortunately, this is far from being the case. Greek Orthodox, Oriental Orthodox, and Catholic denominations, as well as Anglicans and Lutherans, figure among the small and shrinking indigenous Palestinian Christian community. Each of these Christian identities represents the tidal markers from the various waves of foreign Christians who came to the Holy Land in the past—either to pray, to conquer, or to control. More recent foreign pilgrims have included Mormons, Pentecostals, and Evangelical Christian Zionists.

Many of the denominational divisions among Christians in the Holy Land originated or were reinforced by the proselytising activities of foreign Christians serving the interests of rival European powers during the last decades of the Ottoman empire in the 19th century and early 20th centuries.[1] This was part of a broader attempt by European powers to stake out a claim to interfere in the affairs of the Ottoman empire for political and strategic ends. 'What amounted to a French protectorate was established over all the Latin Catholics in the Levant ... France was ahead of its European rivals but not by far. Russia claimed similar protection over the rights of Orthodox Christians in the Empire.'[2] France also fostered the Eastern Catholic communities. Germany sought to be the patron of both Catholics and Protestants, and Germany also gave strong support to the Turks themselves. Britain began by trying to foster an Anglican community through making converts from Judaism. When this proved of limited success, the British managed to proselytise from existing Christian communities. Later, Britain established itself as the protector of all Jews in the Ottoman empire.[3]

Today Christians make up 6.7 percent of the total of Palestinians throughout the world. In the West Bank and Gaza they now number 2.9 percent and in Israel at 2.3 percent of the 14 percent Palestinian community, although the figure is sometimes given as one million—some 20 percent.[4] In Jerusalem, the Christian population more than halved between 1914 and

---

[1] Education played a key role in proselytism of indigenous Christians within the framework of the 'cultural field, in which the Western powers and their co-ordinate religious denominations vied with one another for the hearts and minds of rising Christian as well as Muslim elites.' R Heacock, 'International Politics and sectarian Policy in the Late Ottoman Period', Thomas Hummel *et al.*, eds., *Patterns of the Past and Prospects for the Future: The Christian Heritage in the Holy Land,* Melisende, London, 1999, 30.

[2] P Mansfield, *Arab History of the Middle East,* Viking, London, 1991, 38.

[3] This led easily to the position taken in the Balfour Declaration in 1917, promising a Jewish homeland in Palestine.

[4] D Macpherson, ed., *A Third Millennium Guide to Pilgrimage to the Holy Land*, Melisende, London, 2000, 40-48. Figures for the numbers of Christians in the Holy Land and for their breakdown by denomination are often disputed. Figures in this volume were based upon figures for Christians in the Occupied Territories provided by B Sabella in 'Socio-Economic Characteristics and Challenges', Prior and Taylor, *ibid.*, 38-39. Figures for Israel are taken from the *Israel Yearbook* for 1999, with the figures for Jerusalem subtracted.

1981. Adding together the figures for Israel and the West Bank and Gaza, the Greek Orthodox are the largest Christian community with around 55,000. The Greek Catholics have around 53,000, the Latins more than 38,000, the Maronites 6,000, Anglicans and Lutherans combine to about 3,000 and the Armenians number about 2,000. In addition to the Palestinian Christians living in the Holy Land, other groupings consist of Lebanese and other Arabic-speaking Christians who merge easily into the Palestinian Christian communities. There are also separate communities of Hebrew-speaking Christians.[5]

The Greek Orthodox community is the largest Christian denomination in the Holy Land, numbering 27,000 in Jerusalem and the Occupied Territories and approximately 29,000 in Israel proper. If we exclude Egypt with more than 10 percent of its population adhering to the Coptic Orthodox Church, it is the most numerous of the Christian denominations in the Arab world.[6] Its roots in the Holy Land go back to the time of Emperor Constantine who inaugurated both the Byzantine empire and the established Church in the Holy Land. The Greek Church remained in communion with the Bishop of Rome until the 11th century schism that divided Eastern and Western Christianity.

The Greek Orthodox Patriarch of Jerusalem traditionally has precedence over other Church leaders.[7] The Greek Orthodox follow the teachings of the seven Ecumenical Councils that preceded the break with Rome. Consequently, elements of their doctrine differ from that of Protestant Christians but are shared by Catholics. Thus, Orthodox Christians invoke the saints and venerate their relics and images.[8] They also pray for the dead and have a realist interpretation of the sacraments. However, they

---

[5] There are a number of Hebrew-speaking Christians in Israel adhering to established Reformed and Roman Catholic traditions. There are also around 20,000 'Messianic Jews', Evangelical Christian converts from Judaism, who have accepted Jesus as the Messiah. A further category of Christians living in the Holy Land consists of a growing minority of the population who are Christian but neither Arab nor Jewish. These consist of migrant workers and immigrants from Eastern Europe and elsewhere. Many of these have been accepted as Jewish and have been allowed citizenship by the Israeli authorities but still regard themselves as Orthodox or Catholic Christians.

[6] H Norman, A *Guide to the Christian Churches in the Middle East*, Mission Focus, Elkhart, Indiana, 1989, 96-117.

[7] The patriarch, like most of the other senior clergy, is expatriate Greek, ruling over Arab married parish clergy and laity. By contrast the Greek Orthodox in Jordan and Syria are part of the Patriarchate of Antioch in Damascus with a largely indigenous Arab leadership and clergy (Horner, *op. cit.,* 9-13).

[8] Two-dimensional ikons are used in the East.

do not subscribe to doctrines defined by Roman Catholic popes and councils after the 11th century.[9]

The Oriental Orthodox[10] comprises the Armenian Orthodox Church (with a Jerusalem Patriarch), the Syrian Orthodox Church (with a Patriarch of Antioch, based in Damascus), the Coptic Orthodox Church (with its Patriarch in Alexandria) and the Ethiopian Orthodox Church (with its Patriarch in Ethiopia).[11] Apart from the Armenian Church, their numbers in the Holy Land are small. Members of all four denominations are mainly to be found in Jerusalem and Bethlehem. Their liturgical customs vary as between the four churches, but their shared doctrinal position is based upon recognition of the first three ecumenical councils. Their independent existence goes back to their rejection of what Orthodox and Western Christians accept as the fourth ecumenical council, the Council of Chalcedon (451), which taught that Jesus Christ is one person with both a divine and a human nature. However, the schism probably owed a lot to resentment against the political and cultural hegemony of the Byzantine empire.[12] Like the Catholics and the Greek Orthodox, they invoke the saints and pray for the dead and have a realist understanding of sacraments.

The Eastern Catholic Churches are communities with distinct liturgical traditions which have all, at some point in their history, been out of communion with Rome. Subsequently they have all had that communion restored and at the same time have been allowed a degree of autonomy in areas of liturgy and custom. The most important of these Churches, the Greek Catholic Church (often called the Melkite Church), is the third largest Christian denomination in the Occupied Territories with 2,850 persons and the largest in Israel proper with over 51,000. The Greek Catholic patriarch is the Melkite patriarch of Antioch based in Damascus. In the Holy Land

---

[9] Thus, they do not profess the Roman Catholic formulations on Purgatory or Transubstantiation, the Assumption of Mary, Papal Infallibility or the Immaculate Conception. With the exception of the last two doctrines, however, the substance of their understanding of these subjects is very close to that of the Roman Catholics. In common with other Eastern Christians, they also reject the *filioque* clause in the Creed professed by Western Christians that states belief in the dual procession of the Holy Spirit from the Father *and the Son*.

[10] Once described as 'Monophysites' (believers in the one divine nature of Christ), the term 'Oriental Orthodox' is now preferred.

[11] A further Oriental Orthodox denomination exists in South India.

[12] 'Dissatisfaction in the East with the heavy handed financial and administrative policies of Constantinople meant that separatist movements developed which combined nationalist and religious complaints into a general desire to break away from the centre.' G Regan, *First Crusader: Byzantium's Holy Wars*, Sutton Publishing, Stroud, 2001, 41.

they have archbishops in Jerusalem and in Galilee. The Greek Catholics derive from a split within the Arab Greek Orthodox Patriarchate of Antioch in 1742. They retained the Greek Orthodox liturgy and the right of clergy to marry before ordination. Once again division among Arab Christians was influenced by the activities of foreigners vying for political and cultural influence.[13] Today Greek Catholics are in many ways the most Arab of the Christian Churches and have a long record of affirming Palestinian rights.

The tiny Armenian Catholic, Syrian Catholic, and Coptic Catholic Churches each originate with a schism from a corresponding Oriental Orthodox Church leading to the restoration of full communion with the papacy. By contrast, the Maronite Church has no corresponding independent Eastern Church from which it derives. A largely Lebanese community, the Maronite Church, with its patriarch in Beirut, was independent from the 7th century but re-united with Rome from the time of the Crusades in the 12th. They number around 57,000 in the Middle East and constitute the largest Christian community in Lebanon with around 50,000. In the Holy Land there are about 6,500 Maronites. Many of these are Lebanese in origin, but there were a number of Maronite villages in northern Palestine and some of them survived the events of 1948.

The term Latin Catholics is usually applied to those Catholics, mostly of Greek Orthodox ancestry,[14] who would normally be described as Roman Catholics in countries not familiar with Eastern Rite Catholics. In the Holy Land these Latin or Roman Catholics constitute less than half of the total number of Catholics, comprising around 23,000 in Israel and 15,000 in Jerusalem and the Occupied Territories. The Latin patriarchate, instituted by the Crusaders (1099–1299), was restored in 1847 in response to 19th-century French political influence, and has authority over the Latin Catholics in historic Palestine and in Jordan.[15]

---

[13] For example, in 1882 the White Fathers set up a seminary for the Greek Catholic clergy at the Church of St Anne in Jerusalem on land given to France by the Turks in recognition of French participation in the Crimean War. (G Anawati, 'The Roman Catholic Church and the Churches in Communion with Rome', A J Arberry, ed., *Religion in the Middle East, Volume 1: Judaism and Christianity*, Cambridge University Press, Cambridge, 1969, 367 and 394, and A Schölch, 'Jerusalem in the Nineteenth Century', A Asali, ed., *Jerusalem in History*, Scorpion, London, 1989, 234. Moreover, conversions to the Greek, as to the Latin Catholics from the Greek Orthodox Church were one result of European Catholic missionary penetration.

[14] A O'Mahony, 'The Religious, Political and Social Status of the Christian Community in Palestine c. 1800-1930,' A O'Mahony *et al.*, eds., *The Christian Heritage in the Holy Land*, Scorpion Cavendish, London, 1995, 244.

[15] The present Latin Patriarch of Jerusalem, Patriarch Michel Sabbah, whose family comes from Nazareth, is the first-ever Latin patriarch to be a Palestinian. There is a Latin Catholic

Among the Protestant Churches in the Holy Land, the Anglican Church and Lutheran Churches are the largest and most influential. Like the Catholics, their separate existence in the Holy Land is largely based upon conversions from Orthodoxy brought about in the struggle for influence by Western Christians—in this case the English and the Prussians. It was at first intended, in a scheme drawn up in 1841 at the instigation of King Frederick William IV, that there would be a joint Anglican-Lutheran bishopric, but theological disagreements combined with political tensions between Britain and Prussia led to the collapse of the scheme in 1886.[16] Today the Anglicans are referred to as Evangelical or Episcopal. Both Lutherans and Anglicans are relatively few in numbers, having a combined presence of just under 3,000 in the whole of historic Palestine, but both communities are internationally influential in their advocacy of the Palestinian cause. Other reformed Churches, most notably the Baptist, have gained a foothold in the Palestinian Christian community. The Bible College in Bethlehem represents an important outpost of Evangelical, Protestant Christianity in the Holy Land.

The ecumenical movement in the Holy Land has been hindered by the often chauvinistic attitudes of expatriate Christians concerned with maintaining possession of their own corners of shrines and their own control over their dwindling flocks. Among the Palestinian Christians, however, there is a growing sense of solidarity across denominational lines. This solidarity is fed by a common sense of isolation as a minority among Muslims, themselves a minority under Israeli rule. It is not uncommon to find Orthodox, Anglican and Catholic members within one family, and today this is unlikely to cause much friction.[17]

Palestinian Christians are conscious that they have shared in the sufferings inflicted on the Palestinian people as a whole. Around 50,000 of them became refugees in 1948 (7 percent of the total number of refugees).[18] Others left their homes to escape from discrimination and the ever-present threat of violence. A higher proportion of Christians has emigrated than is

---

seminary in Beit Jala near Bethlehem. Latin Catholics administer the Christian Information Centre near the Jaffa Gate, the Pilgrim Liaison Office at the Notre Dame Centre opposite the New Gate, and an important legal rights centre, the Society of Saint Yves.

[16] T M Hornus 'The Lutheran and Reformed Churches,' Arberry, *op. cit.*, 541. Subsequently Anglicans and Lutherans developed separate episcopates. Today each of the two communities has a Palestinian bishop in Jerusalem.

[17] I have been told by Christian Palestinians that in a situation where educated Palestinian Christians sometimes 'marry out' to find Muslim partners, Christian families are content when their children find Christian spouses whatever their denomination.

[18] Sabella, *op. cit.*, 33.

the case with the Palestinians as a whole. This has been due partly to the high level of education received in Christian schools sponsored by the western churches and partly to the relative prosperity of some Christian Palestinian families.[19]

Having been divided by foreign Christians ambitious to determine the future of the Holy Land, Palestinian Christians today are brought together by their common stake in Palestinian self-determination. Most of the churches in the Holy Land are affiliated to the Middle East Council of Churches. The Palestinian Liberation Theology Center, *Sabeel*, too is ecumenical in character. *Al-Liqa'*, which enjoys the support of Palestinian Christians from different traditions, organises publications and conferences on Christian-Muslim dialogue and on cultural, historical and political issues. Because of the political situation, organisations promoting Jewish-Christian dialogue are supported mainly by expatriate Western Christians.

Clearly, sensitivity to the Christian ecumenical dimension in the preaching of pilgrimage leaders to the Holy Land can help the development of stronger links between the Churches. In the wider worldwide preaching context reference, to the rich variety of Christian witness in the Holy Land can only serve to promote the cause of Christian unity. According to the Acts of the Apostles, it was in the Holy Land that the united Church of Pentecost first put out its roots. A grasp of how political and cultural imperialism helped to produce the scandal of subsequent disunity in the indigenous Church can strengthen historical understanding of the contingent political and cultural causes of division not only in the Holy Land but elsewhere. Likewise an appreciation of the impact of how a shared sense of isolation and adversity can contribute to Christian solidarity among Palestinian Christians may contribute to a growth in solidarity between Christians elsewhere in other circumstances of adversity.

All of the Christian communities are part of a continuous presence in the Holy Land since the time of Christ, and the leaders of all the major denominations try to draw the attention of Western Christians to the implications of their gradual disappearance for the Christian world as a whole. Such is the primary focus of 'Living Stones,' an 'ecumenical trust seeking to promote contacts between Christians in Britain and Christians in the Holy Land and neighbouring countries.'[20] This organisation has involved Christians in Britain from Anglican, Armenian, Free Church, Orthodox, Quaker, and

---

[19] For a study of the reasons for the Christian exodus, see Sabella, *op. cit.*, 41–42.

[20] D Macpherson, 'Introduction. What is Living Stones', D Macpherson, ed., *A Third Millennium Guide to Pilgrimage to the Holy Land,* Melisende, London, 2000, 7–9.

Roman Catholic traditions united by a common commitment to the single objective of building bridges of solidarity with Christians in the lands of the Bible. The preaching of such a message has the capacity to transcend and to heal the tragedy of division both for those who preach and for those for whom the message is preached. Celebration of the Week of Prayer for Christian Unity, taking place against the background of a continuing international focus on events in the Holy Land, might provide a good framework for exploring these themes.

Preaching Plan: John 4, Jesus and the Samaritan Woman[21]
Preparation of the Homily: Process and Strategies

The story of the meeting of Jesus with the Samaritan woman at the well had here been chosen as a preaching text for the Week of Prayer for Christian

---

21 John 4: Now when Jesus learned that the Pharisees had heard, 'Jesus is making and baptizing more disciples than John'—although it was not Jesus himself but his disciples who baptized—he left Judea and started back to Galilee. But he had to go through Samaria. So he came to a Samaritan city called Sychar, near the plot of ground that Jacob had given to his son Joseph. Jacob's well was there, and Jesus, tired out by his journey, was sitting by the well. It was about noon. A Samaritan woman came to draw water, and Jesus said to her, 'Give me a drink.' (His disciples had gone to the city to buy food.) The Samaritan woman said to him, 'How is it that you, a Jew, ask a drink of me, a woman of Samaria?' (Jews do not share things in common with Samaritans.) Jesus answered her, 'If you knew the gift of God, and who it is that is saying to you, "Give me a drink," you would have asked him, and he would have given you living water.' The woman said to him, 'Sir, you have no bucket, and the well is deep. Where do you get that living water? Are you greater than our ancestor Jacob, who gave us the well, and with his sons and his flocks drank from it?' Jesus said to her, 'Everyone who drinks of this water will be thirsty again, but those who drink of the water that I will give them will never be thirsty. The water that I will give will become in them a spring of water gushing up to eternal life.' The woman said to him, 'Sir, give me this water, so that I may never be thirsty or have to keep coming here to draw water.' Jesus said to her, 'Go, call your husband, and come back.' The woman answered him, 'I have no husband.' Jesus said to her, 'You are right in saying, "I have no husband"; for you have had five husbands, and the one you have now is not your husband. What you have said is true!' The woman said to him, 'Sir, I see that you are a prophet. Our ancestors worshiped on this mountain, but you say that the place where people must worship is in Jerusalem.' Jesus said to her, 'Woman, believe me, the hour is coming when you will worship the Father neither on this mountain nor in Jerusalem. You worship what you do not know; we worship what we know, for salvation is from the Jews. But the hour is coming, and is now here, when the true worshipers will worship the Father in spirit and truth, for the Father seeks such as these to worship him. God is spirit, and those who worship him must worship in spirit and truth.' The woman said to him, 'I know that Messiah is coming' (who is called Christ). 'When he comes, he will proclaim all things to us.' Jesus said to her, 'I am he, the one who is speaking to you.' Just then his disciples came.

Unity and serves to illustrate some of the principles set out in this chapter. The element of encounter in the Palestine of Jesus between rival traditions with the same roots and many of the same beliefs and customs seems to be particularly appropriate for a service for Christians from a variety of denominational backgrounds meeting in Britain. The central relevance of the Gospel passage for such an occasion is that the focus on Jesus and the living water he offers is seen as something that transcends secondary differences of belief and ritual.

Thus the primary affective aim of the homily is to encourage an active commitment to Jesus as the one who satisfies the common thirst in those who accept him. The secondary affective aim is to build active concern for the 'Living Stones' of the Holy Land. Not only is their thirst for freedom

---

They were astonished that he was speaking with a woman, but no one said, 'What do you want?' or, 'Why are you speaking with her?' Then the woman left her water jar and went back to the city. She said to the people, 'Come and see a man who told me everything I have ever done! He cannot be the Messiah, can he?' They left the city and were on their way to him. Meanwhile the disciples were urging him, 'Rabbi, eat something.' But he said to them, 'I have food to eat that you do not know about.' So the disciples said to one another, 'Surely no one has brought him something to eat?' Jesus said to them, 'My food is to do the will of him who sent me and to complete his work. Do you not say, "Four months more, then comes the harvest"? But I tell you, look around you, and see how the fields are ripe for harvesting. The reaper is already receiving wages and is gathering fruit for eternal life, so that sower and reaper may rejoice together. For here the saying holds true, "One sows and another reaps." I sent you to reap that for which you did not labor. Others have labored, and you have entered into their labor.' Many Samaritans from that city believed in him because of the woman's testimony, 'He told me everything I have ever done.' So when the Samaritans came to him, they asked him to stay with them; and he stayed there two days. And many more believed because of his word. They said to the woman, 'It is no longer because of what you said that we believe, for we have heard for ourselves, and we know that this is truly the Savior of the world.' When the two days were over, he went from that place to Galilee (for Jesus himself had testified that a prophet has no honor in the prophet's own country). When he came to Galilee, the Galileans welcomed him, since they had seen all that he had done in Jerusalem at the festival; for they too had gone to the festival. Then he came again to Cana in Galilee where he had changed the water into wine. Now there was a royal official whose son lay ill in Capernaum. When he heard that Jesus had come from Judea to Galilee, he went and begged him to come down and heal his son, for he was at the point of death. Then Jesus said to him, 'Unless you see signs and wonders you will not believe.' The official said to him, 'Sir, come down before my little boy dies.' Jesus said to him, 'Go; your son will live.' The man believed the word that Jesus spoke to him and started on his way. As he was going down, his slaves met him and told him that his child was alive. So he asked them the hour when he began to recover, and they said to him, 'Yesterday at one in the afternoon the fever left him.' The father realized that this was the hour when Jesus had said to him, 'Your son will live.' So he himself believed, along with his whole household. Now this was the second sign that Jesus did after coming from Judea to Galilee.

and justice helping to overcome barriers of disunity for themselves, but building solidarity with them can help to overcome division among Christians both in the Holy Land and elsewhere. The Holy Land experience of the preacher here provides an understanding of the geographical and cultural context of the original story. It also provides the opportunity to identify both the scandal of Christian disunity and the welcome signs of the growth of ecumenical relationships in the Holy Land today. Parallels with the domestic ecumenical situation in Britain and elsewhere are then explored.

Preparatory reading focussed upon critical exegesis of the text and upon the nature of the differences between the Samaritans and the followers of the Judaean Jerusalem cult with whom Jesus is identified.[22] The awkwardness of the encounter between Jesus and the woman was based upon notions of pollution,[23] as well as of gender.[24] The close thematic links between this passage and the account of the meeting with Nicodemus was noted. Without explicit reference in the text of the homily, the parallel helped to inform the reference to common Christian baptism.[25] Although 'Jesus speaks strongly of the superiority of the Jewish traditions,' nevertheless, 'his response to the traditional question of the right place of worship, Gerizim or Jerusalem, transcends what the woman might expect from a prophet.'[26] Applied to the ecumenical enterprise, it holds the lesson that a sense of the validity of one's own tradition can go on to the recognition that Jesus can take his followers beyond the temporary causes of their division

Text of Homily
PROBLEMATIC

You may be wondering how appropriate this long section of John's Gospel is for a service in the Week of Prayer for Christian Unity. Well, our experience of Ecumenism is

---

[22] John 4: 9, 20, 22.

[23] 'Since in antiquity people and land were organically connected, it followed that both Samaritans and their land were unclean or impure in Judean eyes.' B Malina and R Rohrbaugh, *Social Science Commentary on the Gospel of John,* Fortress Press, Minneapolis, 1998, 98.

[24] An analysis of teaching on the uncleanness associated with women's menstruation, Samaritan women, and women in relationships outside of wedlock means that 'from the point of view of Judean values … this whole scene appears socially deviant.' Malina and Rohrbaugh, *ibid.,* 99.

[25] M M Pazdan, 'Third Sunday in Lent, Year A', R van Harn, ed., *The Lectionary Commentary: Theological Exegesis for Sunday's Texts. The Third Readings: The Gospels,* Eerdmans, Grand Rapids, 2001, 501-5.

[26] F Moloney, *Sacra Pagina: The Gospel of John,* Liturgical Press, Collegeville, Minnesota 1998, 128-129.

an experience of encounter across barriers. Our friendships are becoming firmly established now, but some of us may remember when meetings between Christians of different denominations were occasions of some embarrassment, when awareness of our differences was much more to the fore than awareness of what we had in common. Listening to the way that the Samaritan woman fenced with Jesus in her conversation at the well, we can sympathise with her embarrassment.

For several reasons, the meeting between the two was a break with convention. Not only was the woman a woman in a culture where women were regarded as a threat to ritual purity, but she was a woman in an irregular relationship. She and Jesus also belonged to rival traditions. The two traditions shared a lot. Like the Samaritans, the Judeans believed in the one God and in five books of Moses. The passage tells us that they also expected the coming of the Messiah. That sounds like a considerable area of agreement, but the differences seemed much greater in the mind both of the woman and of the author of the Gospel. 'How is it that you, a Jew, ask a drink of me, and me a woman of Samaria? Jews do not share things in common with Samaritans.'

That is true today. Those of you who have been to the Holy Land may have visited the Church of Jacob's Well near the Palestinian town of Nablus in the West Bank. Overlooking the town there is Mount Gerizim, where a tiny community of Samaritans celebrates Passover every year. When you go up onto the Mount, you can visit a small museum of Samaritan history. You can also see the place where they sacrifice the animals for this festival—something the Jews have not done since the destruction of the Second Temple in Jerusalem in 70 AD. One of the reasons that the Samaritan community is so small today is that they refuse to intermarry with non-Samaritans. The Samaritans who live on Mount Gerizim refuse to accept Israeli citizenship or to use the Hebrew language except in their services. Now as then 'Jews do not share things in common with Samaritans..'

Another thing you notice when you visit the Holy Land is that the Christians have been keeping each other at arms-length for some time as well. In the Church of the Holy Sepulchre and the Church of the Nativity, different Churches have separate areas for their services—separate altars for which they are responsible. There have been occasions when monks of rival ancient churches have resorted to blows over trespass on disputed sacred ground. Some Evangelical Christians favour a rival Holy Sepulchre in a Garden a mile away from the Church of the Holy Sepulchre.[27] And near Bethlehem there are separate Catholic, Greek Orthodox, and Protestant 'Shepherds' Field'—presumably some of the shepherds in the Christmas story were Catholic and others were Orthodox or Protestant! The rival sites of the Jews and the Samaritans provide a pattern of something in human nature that has not changed!

---

[27] 'The Holy Sepulchre or the Garden Tomb', in A Hilliard and B Bailey, *Living Stones Pilgrimage,* Cassell, London, 1999, 43-45.

GOOD NEWS

Well, the good news is that change is possible. It is possible because people of all kinds need the same things. They need water for a start: 'If you knew the gift of God and who it is that is saying to you, "Give me a drink," you would have asked him and he would have given you living water.' So the woman said to him, 'Sir, you have no bucket, and the well is deep. Where do you get that living water?' She thought he was talking about ordinary water—an understandable mistake. Water is scarce in the Holy Land even today. In October 2002, the Israelis announced measures to forbid the Palestinians in the West Bank from drawing any more water.[28] They said that this was to be a collective punishment for a suicide attack on an Israeli bus, but the use of scarce water resources as a weapon was already well established. But Jesus was talking about the water that human beings thirst for even more than for ordinary water—'Whoever drinks of the water that I will give them will never be thirsty. The water that I will give will become in them a spring of water welling up to eternal life.' The fact that the woman was a Samaritan made no difference. The fact that she was a woman in a world where men did not socialise with women outside their own family circle made no difference. The fact that the woman had a colourful private life made no difference.[29] She was able to recognise Jesus as the Christ and bring other people to him. Those who believed in Jesus needed the same living water and drank from the same living water.

So it is with Christians. Their rival holy places and traditions may divide them, but they are united at the level of their deepest spiritual need. They are united, too, by the gift of God that satisfies that need. The gift transcends the differences between the people who receive it: 'The hour is coming when you will worship the Father neither on this mountain or in Jerusalem … but the hour is coming and now is when those who worship God will worship him in spirit and in truth.'

APPLICATION

So here we are, united by our need and by the gift we have received in answer to that need—united by our faith in Christ and by the living water that we have shared in our baptism. As we apply this truth to our lives, we find that we cannot help growing in unity with each other. Our sisters and brothers in the Churches of the Holy Land have begun to experience this growing together. Oppressed by the political situation in which they find themselves, and with their very survival as a community threatened, the Palestinian Christians have formed bonds of unity through the Middle East Council of Churches. Unlike the case of the Roman Catholic Church in the World Council of Churches, where it has the status of observer, in the case of the Middle East Council of Churches it is a full member, and the Latin patriarch has served as its co-chair. Palestinian

---

[28] *The Guardian*, London, 23 October 2002.
[29] John 4: 16–18.

Christians have formed bonds of solidarity through Sabeel, *an organisation that is trying to develop a liberation theology that speaks to their situation. Palestinian Christians have formed bonds of unity through Al-Liqa', an interfaith organisation that promotes a new dialogue between Christians and Muslims. Their need brings them together, but so too does the gift they have received—their sharing in the living water of Christ.*

Does this connect in any way with us? I would suggest that it does. We can find common purpose in showing support and solidarity for the Palestinians and not least for the Palestinian Christians, the Living Stones of the Holy Land. We can learn too from their experience. We find common purpose in showing support and solidarity for oppressed people everywhere. The encounter with Christ takes us beyond our differences and invites us to experience something quite different. As Jesus said to the Samaritan woman, 'The hour is coming and is now here when the true worshippers will worship the Father.'

Chapter 5
MULTI-FAITH PLURALISM
IN THE HOLY LAND

We saw his star as it rose and have come to do him homage (Matthew 2: 2).

What is true about the important awareness of Christian pluralism in preaching is true also for awareness of the wider pluralism of the three Semitic religions and, by extension, of all religions. One of the primary religious realities of the Holy Land is that it is holy to the three Abrahamic and Semitic faiths: Christianity, Islam, and Judaism. In Israel today there are approximately six million people of whom 81.45 percent are Jews, a further 16.3 percent are Palestinian Muslims and 2.3 percent Palestinian Christian.[1] In the West Bank (including East Jerusalem) and Gaza, there are approximately three million people, a figure that includes 400,000 Jewish settlers and a mere 51,000 Palestinian Christians. Nearly all of the remainder is Muslim Palestinian.[2]

Preachers with a narrowly exclusivist Christian perspective may be able to ignore this reality and concentrate on the significance of the land in terms of biblical sites associated with the Christian story alone. However, many of the sites referred to in the Bible and revered by Christians are also revered by one or other or both of the other two faiths. Those preachers influenced by more inclusivist currents of thinking—for example those of the Second Vatican Council's *Nostra Aetate*[3]—are compelled to provide a homiletic perspective that addresses the significance of some of these sites to Judaism and Islam.

For Jews, the Holy Land is the land promised to Abraham and Moses, the land of David and Solomon. Long before modern Zionism succeeded in giving it political significance, the Holy Land, and Jerusalem in particular, served as a spiritual symbol of religious identity and of eschatological hope for Jews throughout the world.

For Muslims, Jerusalem, al-Quds al-Sharif, is associated with the offering of Ishmael as a sacrifice by Abraham and also with the furthest *qibla*,

---

[1] Figures from *The World Guide. An Alternative Guide to the Countries of our Planet 2001/2002*, New Internationalist Publications, Oxford, 2001, 302.
[2] *Ibid.*, 424.
[3] A Flannery, *Vatican Council Documents*, Dominican Publications, Dublin, 1975, 738-47.

the destination of the prophet Muhammad on his miraculous night journey from whence he is believed to have been taken up into heaven to receive further revelations. [4] There are many other associations with the prophets of Islam in Israel-Palestine, as well as a number of pious associations often shared either with Christianity and/or Judaism.

For each of the three faiths these common associations can and should provide a special impetus towards dialogue and mutual understanding. Preachers can build on inter-faith understanding with appropriate references to these shared associations in their preaching. To do this with any degree of honesty, however, requires reference to the problematic, often bloody, history of relations between these faiths in past centuries—no one faith is above reproach[5]—as well as to the Israeli-Palestinian conflict of the last fifty years.

The Israeli-Palestinian conflict, like the conflicts of earlier centuries includes religious and political factors that are not always directly related. Unfortunately it does not take long for them to become so. Thus, for most Jews today the Jewish state has become 'part of their self-understanding'.[6] Zionism was initially a project of secular Jewish nationalists. Indeed the leader of the founders of the Zionist community of Petah Tiqvah,[7] 'though an observant Jew, was excommunicated (put into *herem*) by the orthodox rabbis of Jerusalem, because it was heresy for Jews to redeem the soil and so to anticipate the Messiah.'[8] Despite this earlier opposition of religious Jews to the Zionist project, 'In recent times no group of Jews is more enthusiastic

---

[4] Other associations with the prophets of Islam include Adam, as well as Jacob, David, and Solomon, who are credited with having contributed to the building and extension of Al-Aqsa (H A R Gibb and J H Kramers, 'Kubbat al Sakhra,' *Concise Encyclopaedia of Islam,* E J Brill, Leiden, 1974, 267-269). Accounts of these associations with the prophets are contained in Jalalu d'Din as-Sayuty, *Al-Masjidu 'l-Aqsa,* trans. J Reynolds, Oriental Translation Fund, London, 1880.

[5] According to the Byzantine chronicler Antiochus Strategos, the Jewish allies of the Persians massacred Christians in 614. In 1009 Muslims under Caliph Hakim, 'the mad,' massacred Christians, and in 1244 Muslim mercenaries fighting on behalf of the Ayyubids engaged in similar bloodletting. More terrible than any of these was the massacre of Muslims and Jews by Christian Crusaders in 1099. In the modern period the emergence of Zionism and the establishment of the State of Israel have been at the cost of the indigenous Muslim and Christian population.

[6] Here and throughout this section I am indebted to Dr Michael Prior for his analysis and references in his 'Speaking Truth in the Jewish-Christian Dialogue,' in D Thomas and C Amos, eds., *A Faithful Presence. Essays for Kenneth Cragg,* Melisende, London, 2003, 327-47.

[7] Petah Tiqva was set up in 1878 and revived in 1882 by the Russian emigration society Bilu. D Jacobs, *Israel and the Palestinian Territories: Rough Guide,* Rough Guides, London, 1998, 101.

[8] N Bentwich, 'Judaism in Israel', Arberry, *op. cit.*, 62.

for the state.'[9] Unsurprisingly then, the issue of Israel and Zionism invariably overshadows Jewish-Christian dialogue. Where the Jews are Israelis and the Christians are Palestinian Arabs, the issue can be said to preclude the possibility of genuine dialogue altogether. As Bishop Kenneth Cragg has wisely observed, theological dialogue separated from justice can be a snare and a delusion.[10]

Today the religious right includes uncompromising Zionists who interpret the setting up of the Jewish state in 1948 and the capture of Jerusalem in 1967 as precursors of the rebuilding of the temple and the coming of the Messiah. Meanwhile a minority of very observant Jews follows the earlier religious opinion that the coming of the Messiah must come before the return to Zion. These traditionalists are opposed on principle to the existence of the State of Israel. It should be borne in mind, however, that Jews across the political spectrum, from ultra-Zionist to anti-Zionist, might belong to either religious or secular groupings.[11]

It is evident that some Western Christians ignore the honourable anti-Zionist currents of Orthodox Jewry and give more or less uncritical support to Israel and its policies towards the Palestinians. A large group of Western Christians, mainly American and other Evangelical believers, are motivated by apocalyptic speculation. For them, the 1967 Israeli conquest of Jerusalem is the fulfilment of biblical prophecy and a presage of the Second Coming of Jesus.[12] Others are motivated by a desire to improve relations with Judaism, even if that excludes consideration of Muslim-Christian relations. At the theological level this can be understood in terms of the special status given to Judaism. Whether Judaism is seen as the Old Covenant fulfilled and superseded by the New, or whether it is seen as the Older Covenant retaining an enduring value in parallel with Christianity,[13] for Christians, Judaism remains

---

[9] M Prior *Zionism and the State of Israel: A Moral Inquiry,* Routledge, London, 1999, 67-102. Prior here traces the evolution of Jewish religious evaluation of Israel and of Zionism from anathema to sacred significance.

[10] K Cragg, *Palestine: The Prize and Price of Zion,* Cassell, London and Washington, 1997, 217.

[11] Zionism was originally an ideology espoused by non-religious Jews. However after the occupation of the West Bank (including East Jerusalem, Sinai, Gaza, and the Golan Heights) in 1967, the majority of religious Jews became supporters of Israel. For a fuller treatment of this topic, see chapter 5 of M Prior, *Zionism and the State of Israel,* Routledge, London, 1999.

[12] Indeed, in response to the refusal of the international community to recognise the Israeli annexation of Jerusalem or to establish embassies there, a particular group of the evangelical constituency has set up a 'Christian Embassy' in Jerusalem. S Sizer, 'Christian Zionism: true Friends of Israel?', *Living Stones,* Autumn 1998, 18.

[13] Sensitivity to 'supercessionalism' influences one influential North American Theologian, Douglas John Hall, to avoid the terms Old and New Testaments in favour of 'Older' and 'Newer Testaments'. D J Hall, as *Professing the Faith: Christian Theology in a North American Context,* Fortress Press, Minneapolis, 1996, 303 and 407.

a special case among the religions of the world. Western Christians are also more vividly aware of past Christian wrongs against Jews than of those committed against Muslims. This lack of even-handedness in approaches to the two religions is often mirrored in Western Christian attitudes to the Israeli-Palestinian conflict and to the status of Jerusalem.[14]

Neither of these approaches takes serious account of the injustice suffered by the Palestinians, whether Muslim or Christian. Michael Prior highlights the historical misunderstandings or falsifications that have been used by some of the Christian participants in the dialogue. Among North American Catholic writers, he cites Father Edward Flannery as a spokesman for the view that Israel is an essential part of Judaism and that 'support for it is a *sine qua non* of the dialogue.'[15] Flannery further characterises criticism of Israel and Anti-Zionism as 'not necessarily, but … almost always a symptom of "the antisemitic virus"'.[16] In contrast he himself sees Israel as having quasi-messianic significance and, as in some degree at least, fulfilling prophecies of the First Covenant that remained unfulfilled by Christianity.[17] Father Robert Drinan, too, argues that Christians should support the State of Israel 'in reparation or restitution for the genocide of Jews carried out in a nation whose population was overwhelmingly Christian.'[18]

Prior catalogues how Flannery and Drinan accept a whole range of distortions and falsifications and omissions of the historical record regarding the exodus of the Palestinians and subsequent events in 1948. In the case of these and other contributors to the Jewish-Christian dialogue, Prior draws attention to the asymmetries in the relationship. On the one hand, Christians are required to say, 'I am sorry for what my Christian forebears and contemporaries have done to Jews. And I am sorry for my own part in it.' Collectively, the Church should observe the Days of Remembrance of the *Shoah*, and the worldwide Christian community should erect a memorial to

---

[14] By contrast, the leaderships of the major Christian Churches have insisted on the special status of Jerusalem, and in common with the Islamic world they have protested against Israeli attempts to claim a special monopoly over it for one religion at the expense of the others. 'Documents on Jerusalem', PASSIA, Jerusalem, 1996.

[15] E Flannery and H Fisher, 'Israel, Jerusalem, and the Middle East,' E Rudin and M. Tannenbaum, eds., *Twenty Years of Jewish-Catholic Relations*, Paulist, Maywah, New York, 1986, 73-86.

[16] *Ibid.*, 82. For a recent discussion of the relationship between anti-zionism and anti-semitism see M Prior, 'Antizionism = Antisemitism?', *Doctrine and Life* 52 July-August 2002, 339-47.

[17] 'Israel, Jerusalem, and the Middle East', 84-5.

[18] R F Drinan, *Honor the Promise,* Doubleday, Cape Town and New York, 1977, xi.

the victims of the *Shoah*.[19] On the other hand, 'There is no question of a collective of Jews acknowledging Zionist responsibility for the catastrophe perpetrated on the Palestinian Arabs precisely in order to establish a Jewish state, and all of this in the authors' own lifetimes.'[20]

These contradictions were evident during the debates of the Second Vatican Council. The impact of Middle Eastern politics on Christian-Jewish and Christian-Muslim relations provided clear evidence of the way in which cultural and political issues can impede the growth of better relations between world faiths. Nowhere more is this the case than in the Holy Land.

It was the political issue of the Israeli-Palestinian conflict that compelled the Council to broaden its discussion on the Catholic Church's relations with the Jews to include consideration of relations with Islam and then with other religions. The inspiration for the discussion of relations with the Jews stemmed from the conviction that, over the centuries, Christian teaching and preaching had contributed to the anti-Semitism that had led in turn to the Nazi extermination of the Jews. The decision to include Islam in the discussion derived directly from political realities of the Middle East.

The proposal to condemn the long-held prejudice that the Jews shared a common guilt for the death of Jesus Christ may have seemed overdue at a distance in time of only sixteen years from the discovery of the extermination camps in Europe. However, it also came only thirteen years after the *Nakba*—the flight and expulsion of some three-quarters of a million Palestinians from their homes. Arabs and Muslims responded with indignation that although such a statement might help Jews and Christians to live together in peace in the West, it would nevertheless advance the cause of Israel.

Representatives of Arab Catholic communities in the Middle East spoke of the dangers of a backlash against Christians in the Middle East. Reassurance was offered that the statement on the Jews was 'a merely religious question, there is no question that the Council will get entangled in those difficult questions regarding the relations the Arab states and the State of Israel, or regarding so-called Zionism.'[21] Further reassurance came with Pope PaulVI's pilgrimage to the Holy Land in January 1964 giving practical expression to just such a pastoral and politically even-handed approach by the Church.

---

[19] W Harrelson and R M Falk, *Jews and Christians: A Troubled Family,* Abingdon, Nashville, 1990, 195-7.

[20] M Prior. Unpublished material.

[21] Speech by Cardinal Bea reported in Xavier Rynne, *The Fourth Session,* Faber and Faber, London, 1966, 22.

In response to further opposition it was finally agreed to enlarge the declaration on the Jews to embrace all the major world religions. Pope Paul VI's first encyclical *Ecclesiam Suam* (August 1964) centred on the theme of dialogue between the Catholic Church and other traditions and belief systems.[22]

The new approach failed to silence all criticism.[23] For most Arabs, it seemed that the wrongs done to the Jews were being acknowledged but that the injustices suffered by the Palestinians were being ignored.[24] Sympathetic statements on Islam did little to alter this. Nevertheless some Muslim commentators appreciated the new, positive attitude towards Islam by the Council. One article in the Beirut newspaper *L'Orient* argued that Arabs should have welcomed the awakening of the Christian conscience to the truth in other religions. 'It is a pity that the fear of Zionist exploitation prevents them from examining its contents ... Islam is presented as a sister religion. The Christian is exhorted to end all disrespect not only to Jews but also to all non-Christians.'[25] In this respect the author considers that Christianity is moving closer to the greater inclusiveness of the Qur'an.

In retrospect, it can be argued that the Council did unwittingly give some encouragement to commentators sympathetic to Zionism. Nevertheless, since the Second Vatican Council there have been many examples of Christian-Muslim solidarity at both the international and the local level that have strengthened relations between the two faiths. Thus, in respect to

---

[22] 'We refer first briefly to the children of the Hebrew people, worthy of our affection and respect, faithful to the religion of what we call that of the Old Covenant. Then to the adorers of God according to the conception of monotheism, the Moslem religion is especially deserving of our admiration for all that is true and good in their worship of God. And also to the followers of the great Afro-Asiatic religions.' *Ecclesiam Suam* (in English as 'The Paths of the Church'), August 1964, para. 107; text at www.rc.net/rcchurch/vatstmts/index/html.

[23] When the revised document was carried on 20 November 1964, Arab reaction followed speedily. A Syrian radio broadcast referred to 'a facelift which would fool nobody.' *Herder Correspondence*, March 1965, 80.

[24] The theologian René Laurentin considered that the Israelis themselves gave credibility to hostile Arab interpretations by themselves claiming that the denial of Jewish responsibility for the death of Christ had a hidden Zionist agenda. One noted Catholic supporter of Israel, revealed just such an agenda when he expressed the hope that the new dialogue would eventually lead to the recognition of the State of Israel by the Church. Oesterreicher suggested that the immoderate attack on the document by the Arab states had 'deprived them of the sympathies which they had enjoyed before, and thus the hearts of Christians turn to the forward-looking (*sic*) State of Israel.' R Laurentin and J Neusner, 'The Declaration on the relation of the Church to non-Christian Religions, *Commentary on the Documents of Vatican II*, Herder, New York, 1966, 303.

[25] *New York Times*, 26 November 1964.

the Holy Land, Roman Catholic and other Christian bodies have expressed common concern over Jerusalem. In 1980, contrary to United Nations resolutions and in total disregard of responsible world opinion, the Israeli Knesset passed the Ceula Cohen law annexing Jerusalem as 'the eternal capital of Israel' and the *de jure* capital of Israel. In the same year, the Central Committee of the World Council of Churches responded,[26] affirming Jerusalem as a city of Christians, Jews and Muslims whose future could not be considered in isolation from the destiny of the Palestinian people. The Holy See protested in similar vein.[27] These and other Muslim and Christian statements about Jerusalem have turned on the idea that Jerusalem is not just a place where human and religious rights must be protected. It is also a place where the three religions should find common ground.

Evidently there has been common ground between Muslims and Christians at the popular level too, particularly in the Holy Land. Some of this can be attributed to the sense of common cause arising from shared suffering.[28] This sense of common cause has not only expressed itself in solidarity but also in inter-faith dialogue. In the 1980s, a small but significant and influential group of Palestinian Muslim and Christians formed *Al-Liqa'* (literally 'The Meeting'), with the aim of discovering more about each other and building upon solidarity to make new openings in inter-faith dialogue between Christianity and Islam.[29]

---

[26] Statement by the World Council of Churches Central Committee on the Israeli Unilateral Action of Annexing East Jerusalem, Geneva, 20 August 1980. 'Documents on Jerusalem', PASSIA, Jerusalem, 1996, 20.

[27] 'It must be understood that the declaration in 1980 that Jerusalem is the 'central and indivisible capital of Israel' is contrary to international law, based as it is on military occupation without the consent of the interested parties or the United Nations and condemned as it immediately was by the Security Council; the fact that almost no countries have moved their embassies to Jerusalem is further proof that the international community rejects the legitimacy of the unilateral declaration.' Address by the Permanent Observer of the Holy See to the United Nations, Archbishop Renato R Martino, concerning Jerusalem, 10 April 1989, 'Documents on Jerusalem', PASSIA, Jerusalem, 1996, 24.

[28] This solidarity had its roots as early as the beginning of the British Mandate in Palestine when Palestinian Christians were actively involved in anti-Zionist Palestinian politics. In 1918, the Muslim-Christian Society (*A1-Jam'iyyah al-Islamiyyah al-Masihiyyah*) had been formed to develop a common front against the encroachment of Zionism on Palestinian rights. Christians generally made up some 20 percent of the membership despite constituting less than 8 percent of the population of Palestine as a whole.

[29] *Al-Liqa'* was launched after a conference on 'Christian-Muslim Arab Heritage in the Holy Land' at Bethlehem University in 1983. In a personal interview, spokesmen for the organisation emphasise that the initiative was not just a Christian initiative but a joint Muslim-Christian Palestinian one.

The Occupation had attempted to split Christians and Muslims, but Muslims had demonstrated that they shared fully in the Christian concern over the decline in the numbers of Christians in the historic Holy Land of Palestine. Nevertheless, the strong sense of unity between Muslim and Christian had not been matched with real insight by members of each community into what members of the other community really believed. In the understanding of *Al-Liqa'*, the time had come for a mutual discovery going beyond mere tolerance and friendship and opening up a real dialogue between Muslim and Christian which it was hoped might ultimately be extended to include Judaism.

As long as the conflict between Israelis and Palestinians remains unresolved, preachers will find an even-handed approach seems difficult to achieve. If inter-faith relations are complicated by politics in Israel-Palestine, inter-faith issues will be complicated by politics for preachers, as well. Nor is it only the politics of the Holy Land that provides such unwelcome complications. There have been conflicts and bloodshed between Christians and Muslims in Indonesia and Nigeria, between Hindus and Muslims in Kashmir, Buddhists and Hindus in Sri Lanka—and, indeed, between Catholics and Protestant Christians nearer to home. None of these unhappy conflicts should prevent honest and politically informed attempts at inclusive preaching in the Holy Land or anywhere else. Despite these difficulties, the preaching plan that follows attempts to utilise the rich resources of the Holy Land to promote an inclusive consciousness of Christians to issues of pluralism.

Preaching Plan: Matthew 2: 1-12 (With Isaiah 60: 1-6, Ephesians 3: 2-3, 5-6)[30] The Coming of the Wise Men (Feast of the Epiphany)
Preparation of the Homily: Process and Strategies

In this homily, the central theme of the way the Epiphany is interpreted is that Jesus Christ is the one in whom all people find their centre and goal. To

---

[30] Matthew 2: 1-12: After Jesus had been born at Bethlehem in Judaea during the reign of King Herod, some wise men came to Jerusalem from the east. 'Where is the infant king of the Jews?' they asked. 'We saw his star as it rose and have come to do him homage.' When King Herod heard this he was perturbed, and so was the whole of Jerusalem. He called together all the chief priests and the scribes of the people, and enquired of them where the Christ was to be born. 'At Bethlehem in Judaea,' they told him 'for this is what the prophet wrote: And you, Bethlehem, in the land of Judah, you are by no means least among the leaders of Judah, for out of you will come a leader who will shepherd my people Israel'. Then Herod summoned the wise men to see him privately. He asked them the exact date on which the star had appeared, and sent them on to Bethlehem. 'Go and

believe this demands that we should recognise that there are no outsiders to his Epiphany and ask of ourselves whether he is at the centre of our hopes and desires.

The form of the homily makes considerable rhetorical use of the poetic power of the first reading from Isaiah, repeating some of the verses in antiphonal fashion. The verses in this reading are taken from the chapters of Isaiah known by scholars as Trito-Isaiah (56-66)[31] and are usually dated after 520 BC.[32] Trito-Isaiah deals with the theme of the new temple and of its new leadership.[33] All this is against a background of social and economic distress.[34] The verses used here picture the temple as the focus of

---

find out all about the child,' he said 'and when you have found him, let me know, so that I too may go and do him homage.' Having listened to what the king had to say, they set out. And there in front of them was the star they had seen rising; it went forward, and halted over the place where the child was. The sight of the star filled them with delight, and going into the house they saw the child with his mother Mary, and falling to their knees they did him homage. Then, opening their treasures, they offered him gifts of gold and frankincense and myrrh. But they were warned in a dream not to go back to Herod, and returned to their own country by a different way.

Isaiah 60:1-6: Arise, shine out, Jerusalem, for your light has come, the glory of the Lord is rising on you, though night still covers the earth and darkness the peoples. Above you the Lord now rises and above you his glory appears. The nations come to your light and kings to your dawning brightness. Lift up your eyes and look round: all are assembling and coming towards you, your sons from far away and your daughters being tenderly carried. At this sight you will grow radiant, your heart throbbing and full; since the riches of the sea will flow to you, the wealth of the nations come to you; camels in throngs will cover you, and dromedaries of Midian and Ephah; everyone in Sheba will come, bringing gold and incense and singing the praise of the Lord.

Ephesians 3: 2-3, 5-6: You have probably heard how I have been entrusted by God with the grace he meant for you, and that it was by a revelation that I was given the knowledge of the mystery. This mystery that has now been revealed through the Spirit to his holy apostles and prophets was unknown to any men in past generations; it means that pagans now share the same inheritance, that they are parts of the same body, and that the same promise has been made to them, in Christ Jesus, through the gospel.

[31] J Blenkinsopp refers to 'the obvious fact' that chapters '56-66 have been added to 40-55.' J Blenkinsopp, 'Second Isaiah-Prophet of Universalism,' P Davies, ed., *The Prophets,* Sheffield Academic Press, Sheffield, 1996, 198.

[32] 'Trito-Isaiah's activity fell between 537 and 521, perhaps about 530.' C Westermann, *Isaiah 40-66,* SCM Press, London, 1966 (new edition, 1996), 296.

[33] 'In Trito-Isaiah's time the return of the exiles was still a matter of expectation. By far the greatest number then, had not returned. The return envisaged by the prophet was to be a miracle.' Westermann, *ibid.,* 296.

[34] 'The temple was still in ruins ... Jerusalem is still an unwalled city ... and the rest of the country has not yet recovered from the effects of the Babylonian devastation ... The wretched economic and social conditions attested are matched by similar allusions in Haggai and Zechariah from the early Persian period.' Blenkinsopp, *op cit.,* 197-8.

new human family with Gentile kings journeying to a Jerusalem where 'God is radiating a dazzling presence from within the city.'[35] The themes of this passage are woven by Matthew into the story of the Magi and have been included in the liturgy of the Epiphany for this reason.[36]

Exegetical reading confirmed the 'central theme of the Magi as models for gentile believers'.[37] Although it is unknown what their religious affiliation was, 'the Magi come from right outside Judaism.'[38] It seems clear, however, that they were astrologers from somewhere in the eastern region of the Middle East.[39] Matthew places Bethlehem as the destination of the wise men, but there is no indication in Matthew's account of Luke's stable.[40] Clearly, however, there is nowhere for pilgrims in Bethlehem to celebrate the visit of the Magi other than at the traditional site of the birth of Jesus in the Church of the Nativity.

The non-Judaic origins of the Magi make the story eligible for a multi-faith eisegesis. The location of the Church of the Nativity also gives imaginative colour to such an interpretation. A few hundred yards from the Church is the Jewish shrine of Rachel's tomb. Nor can pilgrims easily ignore the sound of the Muezzin calling Muslims to prayer from nearby mosques, providing a background sound to the worship in the Church of the Nativity. The Christian preacher in 'uttermost parts of the earth' can draw from this reality also. The preaching of the Epiphany Gospel can usefully stress that Christians draw from the tradition of Judaism and that Muslims share with Christians a reverence for Christ and his Virgin Mother. There is no sentimentalising away of the political situation, however. If the preacher has an obligation to preach a Gospel that is 'good news for the poor, then there is no easy equation to be made between the oppressor and the oppressed, the occupier and the victim of the occupation. Nevertheless, once the preacher has witnessed to this principle, the central theme of the homily

---

[35] C Stuhlmueller, 'Deutero-Isaiah and Trito-Isaiah,' R Brown, *et al.*, eds., *The New Jerome Biblical Commentary,* Geoffrey Chapman, London, 1989, 345.

[36] *Ibid.*, 346.

[37] D Harrington, *Sacra Pagina: The Gospel of Matthew,* Liturgical Press, Collegeville, Minnesota, 1991, 46.

[38] G N Stanton, 'The Communities of Matthew,' in J D Kingsbury, *Gospel Interpretation: Narrative Critical and Social Scientific Approaches,* Trinity Press, Harrisburg, Pennsylvania, 1997, 62.

[39] 'The term "Magi" suggests Persia, their practice of astrology indicates Babylon and the gifts they bring point to Arabia or the Syrian desert.' D Harrington, *op. cit.*, 42.

[40] Harrington points out: 'Matthew seems to assume that Mary and Joseph live in a house at Bethlehem' but goes on to try to harmonise the two accounts by suggesting that Luke's 'stable' may have been a reference to 'the part of a private house set apart for animals that could be used also as guest quarters in an emergency.' *Ibid.*, 43.

can focus on the belief that Christ is the 'desire of the nations,' and the Magi can stand for believers of all the great religions who contrive to follow whatever light they have been given. One verse from the second reading (Ephesians 3:6), is selected to reinforce this theme. The apparent contradiction between dialogue and evangelisation is left unresolved.

Outline Text of Homily
PROBLEMATIC

'Arise, shine out, Jerusalem, for your light has come, the glory of the Lord is rising on you, though night still covers the earth and darkness the peoples.'

The second part of that verse from Isaiah, 'night still covers the earth and darkness the peoples,' certainly rings true, the first part—'your light has come, the glory of the Lord is rising on you,' may seem more problematic. It would have been problematic for the people who first heard these words. This part of the book of Isaiah was addressed to a people who had been in captivity in Babylon. Today there may be other reasons to be gloomy, some of them personal and some to do with the state of the world. Anyone who has been following events in Bethlehem and the surrounding area in recent months and years will have no reason to doubt that 'night still covers the earth and darkness the peoples.' Matthew represents King Herod as a tyrant. Those who have visited or taken an interest in what has been happening in the Holy Land will know that since 1967 the people of Bethlehem have been under the tyranny of a military occupation. The fact that they have had a brief experience of self-rule following peace agreements between Israel and the Palestinians simply makes the destruction and bloodshed of the last year even more tragic. And innocent Israeli civilians have been victims of savage reprisals by Palestinian suicide bombers. 'Night still covers the earth and darkness the peoples.'

Of course, the peoples of the Holy Land are not the only people covered by darkness. In 2002, Chechnya, the Congo, Sri Lanka, Sierra Leone have suffered even more pain and bloodshed. They have been covered by even greater darkness. Here at home, too, night has covered the earth. We have experienced bereavement, family breakdown, sickness and loneliness. 'Night still covers the earth and darkness the peoples.'

GOOD NEWS

However Isaiah gives a command: 'Arise, shine out, Jerusalem.' And it is a command based on hope: 'for your light has come, the glory of the Lord is rising on you.' People living in the east, in Babylon, can expect to come home: 'Lift up your eyes and look round: all are assembling and coming towards you, Your sons from far away and your daughters being tenderly carried.' Jerusalem and its temple will be rebuilt.

And the foreign nations will help them and bring them their treasures: 'Camels in throngs will cover you, and dromedaries of Midian and Ephah; everyone in Sheba will come, bringing gold and incense and singing the praise of the Lord.' So the good news for them was homecoming to a place full of the bright glory of the Lord. And the good news we celebrate today is the Epiphany, the manifestation of the glory of Christ to the gentiles. In our Western part of the Church this refers to the coming of the wise men. The scholars tell us that they may not have been kings and there may not have been three—tradition make them out to be three so that there can be one to carry each of the three gifts of gold, frankincense, and myrrh. What is more certain is that they were gentile astrologers, outsiders to the Jewish nation and the faith of Judaism. They came searching, following the light that was given to them and they found Christ: 'We saw his star as it rose and have come to do him homage.'

And this is good news for us at two levels. It is good news for each individual here because we are the gentiles, the outsiders. Most of us are descended from gentiles, pagans. All of us were outsiders because of our sins. All of us who seek can find. And when we do it, doesn't seem like that at all. It was Christ who came seeking us and we who were found.

It is also good because it means that the child of Bethlehem can break down the walls of division, the barriers between people. All those who sincerely follow the light they have been given but who have not yet found their way to Christ will find him. This is true for all those who worship God in the great religions of the world and for all those who do not know God but who follow the light of their conscience. God meets people where they are, and there are truths in all the world religions. All religions deserve our respect. This insight, confirmed by the Second Vatican Council, does not mean that we can be apathetic on the grounds that everyone will find Christ in heaven eventually. We may still hope that the true light they have received will bring them to faith in Christ while they are on this earth. 'The sight of the star filled them with delight, and going into the house they saw the child with his mother Mary, and falling to their knees they did him homage.' Who could want to deprive any one the delight of being led to Christ and to be given the opportunity to worship him? As St Paul says of the Jews, the same promise has been made to them, in Christ Jesus, through the gospel.'

APPLICATION

Recognising that Christ is the way to the Father, the centre to which everyone may come challenges me. Am I giving priority to the spiritual search? Do I live like someone who believes that Jesus is the king and centre of all hearts? Do I try to break down barriers between people? Do I respect those who are true to the light they have been given even if that does not make them members of the Church? God does not discriminate against outsiders and strangers. I was an outsider, and he has brought me home to the home I never knew I had. I was a stranger, and he chose me as a friend.

'Arise, shine out, Jerusalem, for your light has come. The glory of the Lord is rising on you. Though night still covers the earth and darkness the peoples.'

Chapter 6
PREACHING IN THE CONTEMPORARY CONTEXT OF THE HOLY LAND WITH SPECIAL REFERENCE TO THE ARAB-ISRAELI CONFLICT

When you see Jerusalem surrounded by armies then you must realise that it will soon be laid desolate (Luke 21: 20).

The modern Christian pilgrim experiences a constant tension between faith in the Prince of Peace and the ever-present reality of violence and the threat of violence between Israelis and Palestinians. This is a tension between belief that the 'light has come' and the evidence, so near to hand, that 'night still covers the earth and darkness the people' (Isaiah 60: 1). The pilgrim and the preacher have the option of ignoring the issue and concentrating on the purely 'spiritual' character of the Holy Land. For those who take this option, understanding of the historical and the political issues underlying the conflict between Israelis and Palestinians is of secondary importance, and seeking to understand the issues is always conditional upon maintaining a position of strict neutrality between the contending parties. Such an approach seems to this writer both to be morally shallow and to betray a weak understanding of the doctrine of the Incarnation.

The alternative approach requires the preacher to face the challenge of doing justice to the issues of the Israeli–Palestinian conflict. This involves the examination of controversial questions requiring historical judgements. For this reason much of this chapter is given over to a somewhat lengthy summary of the forces and events that should inform such judgements.

The summary to follow will indicate that the conflict between the Israelis and the Palestinians is a clash of two nationalisms. It will be seen that in both cases, the intrusion of religious issues into the discourse is a later development. In tracing the course of the conflict, it will be helpful to identify the reasons for this intrusion and to analyse its effect upon the ideology of both parties. Historically Zionism established itself as major political force earlier than did Palestinian nationalism, and religious Zionism preceded the emergence of Islamic political ideology into the Palestinian movement. For this reason the summary, although thematic in structure, proceeds as a largely chronological treatment of events.

Relating judgements on these events to preaching tests both the role and the limits of committed political theology, not only in the Holy Land, but also throughout the world.

At the conclusion of the summary, Christian perspectives on the struggle, some of which have already been discussed in the previous chapter, will be examined. A political hermeneutic then will be suggested that combines commitment to peace and justice with an adequate appreciation of the complicated historical background to the conflict. Finally, a preaching plan will be proposed that seeks to embody such an approach.

Regina Sharif has demonstrated that the earliest proponents of the concept of a Jewish state in Palestine were gentiles rather than Jews. She goes on to categorise the premises of these non-Jewish 'Zionists' variously as those influenced by Christian millenarianism (the belief in the thousand year rule of Christ upon earth), the Romantic movement, and anti-semitic racism.[1] Although not the originator of the idea of a Jewish state,[2] Theodor Herzl (1860-1904) is rightly regarded as the founder of Jewish Zionism[3] as an effective political movement.[4]

In the climate of a rising tide of nationalism in Europe, Herzl became preoccupied with the persistence of anti-semitism and observed that it was directed equally against assimilated and religiously observant Jews. Nationalist ideologies depended upon clear notions of identity—ethnic, cultural, and religious. Such definitions not only strengthened bonds between those who were seen as belonging to the nation, but also served to exclude those who were not. Jews were seen as cosmopolitan outsiders, having no real roots or part in the family of the nation. In the face of this developing hostility, religious Jews retreated into the devout study of Talmud and Torah while numbers of other, secular Jewish intellectuals responded by espousing internationalist-socialist reformist and revolutionary movements. Herzl, by

---

[1] R Sharif, *Non-Jewish Zionism, Its Roots in Western History*, Zed Books, London, 1983, 22-43.

[2] Forerunners of Zionism include Rabbi Yehuda Alkali and Zevi Hirsch Kalisker in the 1860s and, more importantly, Leon Pinsker (1821-1895) who regarded assimilation as an impossibility and favoured a Jewish homeland, although not necessarily in Palestine. H Küng, *Judaism*, trans. J Bowker, SCM Press, London, 1992, 284.

[3] The term 'Zionism' was coined by Nathan Birnbaum in 1891 in his journal *Self Emancipation* that later appeared with the title *An Organ of the Zionists*. 'From the beginning Zionism was not understood in a practical philanthropic sense, but specifically in party political terms.' *Ibid.*, 283.

[4] Herzl produced the first draft of his seminal *Der Judenstaat* in 1895, and the first article propounding his vision was published in the London *Jewish Chronicle* in the following January.

contrast, countered the exclusivism of European nationalisms with its mirror image in a specifically Jewish nationalism.[5] Herzl regarded all Jews as one nation and considered anti-semitism as an inevitable consequence of that fact.[6] The creation of a Jewish state in Palestine[7] would not only fulfil the just aspirations of the Jewish nation but also would serve the interests of other nations whose governments could be expected to give their support to the project as a colonial bastion against Asiatic barbarism.[8]

Although Herzl hoped for support from religious Jews and was sensitive to the power of religious symbolism in Jewish national identity, his vision of a Jewish state was a secular one and was greeted with hostility by most religious Jews.[9]

Undeterred by such opposition, Herzl pressed on with canvassing support for the Zionist project, unsuccessfully soliciting the support of the imperial and royal heads of Europe, the Ottoman sultan and the pope. The British government was rather more positive, and Prime Minister Joseph Chamberlain suggested that a Jewish state be established in Uganda rather than Palestine, a plan briefly entertained by the Zionist movement.[10]

The primary goal of Palestine as a Jewish homeland presented, of course, one important problem—its existing indigenous population. Herzl's diary for 12 June 1895 suggests the solution: 'We shall endeavour to expel the poor population across the border unnoticed, procuring employment for it in the transit countries, but denying it any employment in our own

---

[5] 'Herzl's Zionism had much in common with 'Pan-Germanism', with its emphasis on *das Volk*: all persons of German race, blood or descent, wherever they lived, owed their primary loyalty to Germany, the *Heimat*. Jews, wherever they lived, constituted a distinct nation, whose success could be advanced only by establishing a Jewish nation-state.' Prior, *op. cit.*, 1999, 9.

[6] T Herzl, *The Jewish State*, Dover Editions, New York, 1988, 75-8.

[7] Argentina was also briefly considered as a possible candidate for the location of the new state. M Gilbert, *Israel: A History*, Doubleday, London and New York, 1998, 16.

[8] T Herzl, *The Complete Diaries of Theodor Herzl*, vol. 1, ed., R Patain, trans. H Zohn, Herzl Press, New York, 1960, 96.

[9] 'Many Reform leaders thought of Jewish Nationalism as a betrayal of universalism ... Many Orthodox thinkers shared the Reform suspicion of a revival of Jewish Nationalism and they added the fear that a return to the Holy Land by human effort amounts to a denial of the Messiah for whose coming Jews are to wait patiently.' L Jacobs, *The Jewish Religion: A Companion*, Oxford University Press, Oxford, 1995, 625. Minority exceptions to this trend included Solomon Schechter, a pioneer of Conservative Judaism and the religiously Orthodox Zionist *Misrachi* movement, founded in 1902.

[10] A colony initially for one million Jews would be set up, having a Jewish government, but owing loyalty to the British Crown. Gilbert, *op. cit.*, 21-2.

country.' He added that both 'the process of expropriation and the removal of the poor must be carried out discreetly and circumspectly.'[11]

In the years following between the death of Herzl and the beginning of the First World War, Zionists worked to establish a sense of Jewish nationhood in Palestine itself. Immigrants came from a variety of countries and spoke a variety of languages, and a significant proportion were religious Jews whose presence in Palestine was not in any way associated with Zionism. Hebrew was established as the medium of communication, and in 1909 Tel Aviv ('Hill of Spring') was established as the first exclusively Jewish city, and a Jewish hospital was opened in Haifa and Jerusalem.[12] Between 1901 and 1914, Jewish migrants to Palestine numbered 30,000. This compares with 25,000 between 1880-1900 and 10,000 for 1840-1860.[13] By 1914 there were 90,000 Jews living in Palestine, of whom 75,000 were immigrants.[14]

The 1914-18 War presented the Zionist movement with its first great opportunity. Turkey declared on the side of the Central Powers and, despite the parallel strategy of supporting Pan Arab nationalism at the expense of Turkey,[15] the Sykes-Picot Agreement of January 1916[16] envisaged a division of interest between France and Britain with most of Palestine coming under international administration.

In 1917, Britain made the first major commitment towards the achievement of Zionist ambitions: 'His Majesty's Government view with favour the establishment in Palestine of a national home for the Jewish people and will use their best endeavours to facilitate the achievement of

---

[11] Prior, *op. cit.,* 1999, 98, offers his own translation of 'Die arme Bevölkerung trachten wir unbemerkt über die Grenze zu schaffen, indem wir in den Durchzugsländern Arbeit verschaffen aber in unserem eigenen Lande jederlei Arbeit verweigern,' Vol. II: 117-8, in preference to Zohn's translation, 'We shall try to spirit the penniless population …,' T Herzl, *op. cit.,* 1960, 1: 87-8. Prior further points out that Herzl's diaries were held by the Zionist Movement and that until 1960 only edited versions were released, carefully omitting his 'population transfer' plans.

[12] Gilbert, *op. cit.,* 27-8.

[13] J Lestschinsky, 'Jewish Migrations: 1840-1956', L Finkelstein, *The Jews: Their History Culture and Religion,* vol. 2, Peter Owen, London, 1961, 1554.

[14] Gilbert, *op. cit.,* 30.

[15] Sir Henry McMahon, the British High Commissioner in Egypt, in a letter to Husain ibn 'Ali, the Sharif of Mecca, dated the 24 October 1915, undertook that, with the exception of 'Mersina and Alexandretta and portions of Syria lying to the west of Damascus, Homs, Hama and Aleppo … Great Britain is prepared to recognise and support the independence of the Arabs in all the regions within the limits demanded by the Sheriff of Mecca.' Walter Laqueur, ed., *The Israeli Arab Reader: A Documentary History of the Middle East Conflict,* Weidenfeld and Nicolson, London, 1969, 16-7.

[16] *Ibid.,* 26-32.

this object, it being clearly understood that nothing shall be done which may prejudice the civil and religious rights of existing non-Jewish communities in Palestine or the rights and political status enjoyed by Jews in any other country.'[17]

It is worth pointing out that the non-Jewish communities referred to in the declaration constituted 670,000 Arabs as against 60,000 Jews (9.7 percent of the population, owning only 2.04 percent of the land).[18] It later became clear that nothing being done to 'prejudice the civil and religious rights of existing non-Jewish communities in Palestine' did not mean that the Arab 83 percent of the population would be allowed any part in the exercise of national self-determination.

In 1922, the League of Nations granted Britain a mandate to rule over Palestine that lasted until the setting up of the State of Israel in 1948. Zionist immigration increased.[19] This produced consequent discontent on the part of Arab peasants who were moved from the land following the sale of property by Arab landowners to Jewish settler organisations.

Over the period of the Mandate, the British administration had to cope with pressure and violence from both Jews and Arabs. This combined with the lobbying of states and organisations and the ideological divisions among British politicians and administrators to produce an inconsistent policy in Palestine that pleased nobody. Britain made concessions to the Arabs in 1930, and in the Passfield White Paper of October 1930 noted the evictions of Palestinian peasants from land sold to Zionist settlers. It also emphasised that British commitment to a Jewish homeland in Palestine was conditional upon respect for the rights of those living there already.[20] Under pressure, Britain then retreated from this position.[21] The persecution of the Jews in Europe after the Nazis came to power in Germany in 1933 led to increased Jewish immigration into Palestine, panicking the Palestinians into armed revolt (1933-36). During the revolt, the Peel Commission, reporting in 1937,

---

[17] Secretary of State for Foreign Affairs, Arthur James Balfour, Letter to Lord Rothschild of 2 November, 1917. *Ibid.*, 18.

[8] W Khalidi, *Palestine Reborn*, Tauris, London and New York, 1992, 21.

[19] In 1914, there were no more than 50,000 Jews in Palestine. This figure rose by 147,502 between 1931 and 1935, by 75,510 between 1936 and 1939, and by 35,000 between 1940 and 1942. By 1945, the total Jewish population was 400,000. Finkelstein, *op. cit.*, 1554 and 1557.

[20] R John and S Hadawi, *The Palestine Diary: Vol. I, 1914-1945*, The Palestine Research Centre, Beirut, 1970, 228-32.

[21] In the letter of February 13, 1931, (referred to by the Arabs as the 'Black Letter'), from Prime Minister Ramsay Macdonald to Chaim Weitzmann. Laqueur, *op cit.*, 50.

recognised the impossibility of reconciling the interests of both communities and proposed the partition of Palestine with compulsory population transfer.[22] The Zionist leadership accepted this proposal as a first step, but it seemed a compromise too far for more extreme factions of the movement who regarded it as a betrayal of their vision for a Greater Israel on both banks of the River Jordan.[23]

Meanwhile the Palestinian leadership considered the proposals to constitute an unjust infringement of their fundamental rights leading the exiled Grand Mufti Haj Muhammad Amin Husaini (1893-1976) to the ill-advised course of holding conversations with the Nazi leadership in Berlin.[24] The British then proposed a unitary state of Palestine to become independent in ten years. In this state, the interests of both communities would be safeguarded. In the meanwhile, immigration and land sales would be restricted.[25] This policy was to lead the Zionists to seek support from the United States.[26] From February 1944 onwards, the Irgun[27] declared war on the British in Palestine and widened their campaign of terror against Arabs to include the British personnel.

The end of the Second World War created circumstances favourable to the Zionists. A half million Jewish refugees who had survived the *Shoah* were searching for a home, and finding that immigration to the United States and most other possible destinations was severely restricted. An Anglo-American plan to take in 150,000 each, with the other 200,000 being absorbed by other countries including Argentina, South Africa, and Australia was blocked by American Zionists. The more extreme, rejectionist Zionist groups conducted a campaign of terror against both Britain and the Palestinians, culminating in the blowing up the King David Hotel on 22 July 1946[28] and

---

[22] *Ibid.*, 56-8.

[23] *Ibid.*, 58-61.

[24] Ibid, 80-4.

[25] See the White Paper of 17 May 1939, *Ibid.*, 58-61.

[26] This bid for American support was expressed at a conference sponsored by the Emergency Council of the Zionist Organisation of America held at the Biltmore Hotel in New York in May 1942. The resulting resolutions became known as the 'Biltmore Programme.' R P Stevens, *American Zionism and US Foreign Policy: 1942-7,* Institute for Palestine Studies, Pageant Press, New York, 1962, 3-6.

[27] The Irgun Zvai Leumi (National Military Organisation), formed in 1931, adhered to the Revisionism of Vladimir Jabotinsky (1880-1940), rejecting all compromises falling short of the establishment of a Jewish state on both banks of the River Jordan. The Stern Gang of Avram Stern (1907-42) emerged after a factional dispute in the organisation in 1940.

[28] Casualties included twenty seven British, forty one Palestinian Arabs, seventeen Jews and five others.

the kidnapping and murder of two British sergeants on 30 July 1947.[29] In the meanwhile, the mainstream Zionist leadership proposed a partition-plan envisaging a Jewish state comprising Galilee, the Negev, and the Golan Heights, with a corridor to the sea at Jaffa. In a climate characterised by international sympathy for the tragedy that had befallen European Jewry and an economically weak and morally exhausted Britain, the fulfilment of Herzl's dream was at hand. The combination of Zionist terror and the continual pressure of an American administration, upon whose largesse Britain was now economically dependent, proved irresistible. On 18 February 1947, the British government announced its intention to terminate the Mandate and to leave without delay and on 15 May 1948 handed over all responsibility to the United Nations.

The United Nations recommended a partition plan that would have awarded 57 percent of the land to a Jewish state.[30] The Arabs rejected a division of territory that would have given more than half of Palestine to a community constituting only a third of the population and possessing legal ownership to less than 75 percent of the land.[31]

In the violence that ensued, Zionist forces quickly established the military ascendancy. During the period of the disintegration of British control, Zionist forces set out to establish military control over the areas assigned to a Jewish state in the United Nations Partition Plan. In addition they proposed to seize as much Arab territory and to expel as many Palestinians as possible.[32]

Meanwhile members of the *Irgun* (led by future Prime Minister Menachem Begin) and the Stern Gang (co-led by future Prime Minister Yitzhak Shamir) massacred the Palestinian population of Deir Yassin, near Jerusalem, killing an estimated 245 people, including many women and children.[33] This event, along with other lesser atrocities, provoked terror

---

[29] A total of 338 British subjects were killed by Zionist terrorists during the last three years of the mandate. N Bethel, *The Palestine Triangle*, Andre Deutsche, London, 1979, 361.

[30] At this date Jews constituted only one-third of the population (some 500-600,000 Jews against some 1.4 million Palestinians) and owned 6.6 percent of the total ownership of Palestine. Prior, *op. cit.*, 1999, 23. Lestschinsky, gives a higher figure of 715,000 Jews, L Finkelstein, *op. cit*, 1580.

[31] Prior, *op. cit.*, 1999, 25.

[32] The strategy consisted of massive surprise attack on the civilian populations, prepared for by mortar and rocket bombardment. Clandestine Haganah radio stations broadcast threats of dire punishment in Arabic and advised escape. Prior, *op. cit.*, 1999, 25.

[33] 'The official account written in 1961 by Lieutenant-Colonel Netanel Lorsch, who had fought in the war … describes how Irgun and Stern Gang forces massacred hundreds of villagers, took the rest prisoners and paraded them proudly through the streets of Jerusalem.' Gilbert, *op. cit.*, 169.

among the Palestinian population of the area and provoked a refugee exodus.[34] Hundreds of thousands more were driven out of the Jewish controlled areas by the Jewish brigades. On the 14 May 1948, the State of Israel was declared.

In the war that followed Israel gained control of 78 percent of former mandated Palestine. The West Bank and East Jerusalem were held by Arab forces and came under Jordanian control, while Egypt held Gaza. New Jewish immigrants were to be the lifeblood of the newly independent State of Israel, and in July 1950, on the sixty-fifth anniversary of Herzl's death, the government enacted the Law of Return. Under this law, every Jew anywhere in the world had the right to immigrate into Israel and to obtain citizenship.[35]

For the displaced Palestinians, there was no right of return. For them the Israeli War of Independence was the *Nakba* or disaster. By the time the hostilities ended in February 1949, it is estimated that more than 700,000 Palestinians had become refugees. An estimated 385 to 418 of abandoned Palestinian villages had been destroyed, leaving one hundred Palestinian villages intact.[36] The total number of refugees comprised two thirds of the total number of Palestinian Arabs, of whom 650,000 were Muslim and the remainder Christian (35 percent of the total number of Palestinian Christians). The majority of Palestinian refugees were accommodated in camps in neighbouring Arab countries, in the Jordanian occupied West Bank, or the Egyptian-occupied Gaza strip. There were, in addition, a further category of refugees who were internal exiles, living in Israel as displaced persons but unable to return to their homes.[37] Further expulsions included the forced transfer of the population of 2,700 in Ascalon to Gaza in 1950 and the expulsion from the Negev of 17,000 Bedouin between 1949 and 1950 and a further 7,500 in 1951.[38]

United Nations Resolution 191 urged the right of the refugees to return to their homes and to be compensated for property loss or damage. Otherwise they could be compensated and assisted in resettlement in another country. This was only the first of a number of United Nations

---

[34] B Morris, *The Birth of the Palestinian Refugee Problem: 1947-49*, Oxford University Press, Oxford, 1987, 115.

[35] Those judged a danger to public health and security were excluded, and a later decision also excluded Jews who had converted to Christianity. Gilbert, *op. cit.,* 270.

[36] Determining the precise number of villages destroyed is complicated by the fact that some of these villages were the settlements of migratory Bedouin tribes. Uri Davis, *Israel: An Apartheid State,* Zed Books, London and New Jersey, 1987, 18.

[37] M Tessler, *A History of the Israeli-Palestinian Conflict*, Indiana University Press, Bloomington and Indianapolis, 1974, 281.

[38] N Masalha, *A Land Without a People,* Pluto, London, 1997, 11.

resolutions disregarded by successive Israeli governments. Approximately 150,000 Palestinians who remained in the Jewish state were subject to military law, land confiscation,[39] and a denial of the rights accorded to Jewish Israeli citizens.[40]

Palestinian nationalism, like its Zionist enemy, was born out of the experience of injustice and marginalisation. The process of dispossession and oppression give rise to a distinctively Palestine political consciousness. Long before the emergence of a Palestinian nationalism, however, Palestinian political consciousness had existed as part of a much broader current of Arab nationalism. Inspired by opposition to the Turkish policy of Ottomanisation introduced in 1865, by which non-Turkish subjects of the empire were expected to assume a new, Ottoman identity, Arab nationalists fell into two groupings. The first were those 'who called for Arab Independence within the Ottoman empire and those who insisted upon total independence from the Turks. It should be noted that Palestinian political activists were involved in both nationalist groups.'[41]

To some degree, this Arab nationalism was just one example of a rising tide of nationalism of which European nationalisms, Zionism, and Turkish nationalism were also examples. The revolts against Istanbul and the subsequent regime of Mohammed 'Ali Pasha (1805-1848) aided by his capable son, Ibrahim Pasha (d. 1848), had sought to promote the values of secular liberalism. These values were to become further fashionable through the influence of western Christian schools, increasingly involved in the education of the children of the Arab elites. The relationship between enlightenment values and nationalism is a complicated one, but the linkage had additional power in the case of nationalist opposition to the Ottoman empire, which was seen as decadent and held back by religious obscurantism.

---

[39] Over 80 percent of the lands of those who never left their homes have been confiscated since 1948, for the exclusive disposal of the Jewish citizens of the state. Today 92 percent of the area of the State of Israel is exclusively for Jews compared with a figure of 7 percent of land purchased legally prior to 1948. W Khalidi, ed., *All That Remains: The Palestinian Villages Occupied and Depopulated in Israel*, Institute for Palestine Studies, Washington, D.C., 1992, xxxii.

[40] See E T Zureik, *The Palestinians in Israel: A Study in Inner Colonialism*, Routledge and Keegan Paul, London, 1979. Military government of the Palestinians inside the State of Israel ended as late as 1 December 1966. Palestinians in Israel now number nearly one million.

[41] Thus, in 1914 the Arab Revolutionary Society called upon all Palestinians, whether Muslim, Jewish, or Christian to unite in resistance. A Ayyad, *Arab Nationalism and the Palestinians*, PASSIA, Jerusalem, 1999, 7.

As the Zionist settlement of Palestine increased, politicised Palestinians voiced their opposition initially as part of a secular Arab movement against Turkish domination.[42] By 1927, however, with the Turks gone and Zionist settlement increasing, the Palestinians were beginning to re-evaluate their relationship with the wider Arab movement.[43] During the next two decades the absence of effective Arab support for the Palestinian cause and the ineffectiveness of the traditional Palestinian leadership became evident with each new calamity. The rise of Nasserism in Egypt revived pan-Arab expectations somewhat, and the Anglo-French Suez debacle of 1956 gave it greater credibility. With the war of 1967, however, the Palestinians experienced their second *Nakba*, and the ineffectiveness of support from the Arab nations was exposed.

After the war of 1967, a further 300,000 Palestinians were driven out or fled from the West Bank, including 100,000 refugees from the camps outside Jericho. In addition, some 100,000 Syrians were evicted from the Golan, leaving only four Druze villages, inhabited today by around 16,000. The villages of Bayt Nuba, 'Imwas, and Yalu in the Latrun salient, as well as the villages of Bayt Marsam, Bayt 'Awa, Habla, and Jifliq, were razed and their inhabitants driven out. Five thousand Jerusalem Arabs were expelled from Jerusalem. Six hundred and fifty of these had lived in the 135 houses in the Moroccan Quarter of Jerusalem destroyed by the Israelis to create an open vista in front of the Western Wall. A further 4,000 Arabs were expelled from Jerusalem's Jewish Quarter occupied by Palestinians since the war of 1948. Bedouin communities in the Rafah salient were also evicted in favour of new Jewish settlements.

Despite United Nations Resolution 242 of 22 November 1967 calling for the return of the territory occupied in the war, Israel continued its occupation. Further, during the period of the Labour-led governments of 1967-77, East Jerusalem was annexed and, as a consequence of the July 1967 Allon Plan, formulated to plant Jewish settlements in the occupied territories, one third of the West Bank was taken into Israeli ownership.

Meanwhile the Palestine Liberation Organization (PLO) and the Palestine National Council (PNC) had been founded in Jerusalem in May 1964 and a Palestinian national covenant approved. The PLO Charter called for a united secular state of Palestine, with Jewish right to citizenship based upon residence in Palestine before 1946.

---

[42] N Masalha, *op. cit.*, 58.
[43] *Ibid.*, 115.

In the first period of Palestinian nationalism there was a major emphasis on guerrilla tactics. And by early 1970, there were at least seven Palestinian *fida'in*, or guerrilla organisations, in Jordan, *all* loosely integrated into the PLO under Yasser Arafat (b. 1929), leader of the dominant *Fatah,* which he had headed since its formal inception in 1963. The first guerrilla attack followed in December 1964.[44] Among the most radical of the guerrilla groups was the Popular Front for the Liberation of Palestine (PFLP) led by George Habash. A more ideologically Marxist faction under the leadership of Nayef Hawatmeh then split from the PFLP to become the Popular Democratic Front for the Liberation of Palestine (PDFLP).

Jordan became the main base for guerrilla actions, and these provoked reprisal attacks by Israeli forces. In March 1968, an Israeli column invaded Jordanian territory and received a bloody repulse at Karameh. Despite the shared euphoria of Palestinians and Jordanians over the battle, King Hussain resented military adventures that provoked Israeli incursions into his territory. He also perceived the PLO as constituting 'a state within the state' and thus as a threat to his authority.

After unsuccessful attempts to disarm the Palestinians and to suppress independent Palestinian military action, King Hussein proved equally unsuccessful in establishing a peace settlement with the Palestinians. Meanwhile, armed confrontations occurred between Palestinian militia and Jordanian forces. On 6 September, members of George Habash's Popular Front for the Liberation of Palestine hijacked three airliners and attempted to hijack a fourth.

King Hussein again ordered the PLO to surrender their arms, and his forces invaded the refugee camps to impose Jordanian state authority. There then followed the fierce ten–day war remembered as 'Black September' which cost an estimated 3,000 Palestinian and 500 Jordanian lives. Syria and Iraq came close to being directly involved on the Palestinian side, and the United States and Israel were close to being implicated in support of King Hussein. After several abortive agreements between Hussein and Arafat and further armed confrontations, the PLO had been effectively neutralised in Jordan.

With the Palestinian leadership powerless, radical groups operating within the PLO, but not under the control of the leadership, engaged in a series of terrorist operations. In November 1970 the newly formed 'Black September' group assassinated Jordanian Prime Minister Tal in Cairo. Subsequent outrages included, most notoriously, in May 1971 the PFLP-sponsored attack on Lod Airport in which 27 Italian pilgrims were killed by

---

[44] J Gee, *Unequal Conflict: The Palestinians and the Israelis*, Pluto Press, London, 1998, 91.

three Japanese terrorists and then, in September 1972, the massacre of Israeli athletes at the Munich Olympic Games. Israel responded by forming a 'Wrath of God' group to assassinate Palestinian leaders.

In October 1973, Egypt and Syria attempted to recover lost territory. Israel suffered initial reverses in the Sinai in the Golan until a massive airlift of arms to Israel from America helped Israel to recover the advantage. Backed by an Arab oil boycott Yasser Arafat tried a diplomatic initiative and addressed the United Nations calling for a united Palestine with a democratic and secular government for all. It was on this occasion that Arafat uttered his famous line, 'I come to you with an olive branch and a freedom fighter's gun; do not let the olive branch fall from my hand.' The PLO was recognised by the United Nations General Assembly as the representative of the Palestinian people (Resolution 3210) on 14 October 1974, with observer status.

Relocated in Lebanon, in 1975 the PLO became embroiled in the Lebanese civil war and, in response, Israel made its first incursion into the Lebanon in March 1976, advancing as far as the Litani river. In 1977 Menachem Begin, the former Zionist terrorist leader, became Prime Minister and in 1978 concluded the Camp David Accords with Egypt, and Israel evacuated the Sinai. In June 1982, Israel engaged in a full-scale invasion of the Lebanon to destroy the PLO and advanced as far as Beirut. Eventually the PLO fighters were allowed to leave, and Arafat moved his headquarters to Tunis. Israel's Christian militia allies then proceeded to massacre large numbers of Palestinian civilians in the refugee camps of Sabra and Shatilla with the active collusion of the Israeli Defence Forces. In 1983 Yitzhak Shamir, a former terrorist, was elected as Prime Minister.

In 1987, the Palestinian population in the West Bank and Gaza began a popular uprising, or *Intifada* ('after-shock'), against the occupation, and in 1988 Jordan abandoned its claim to the West Bank. In the same year the PLO initiated another diplomatic initiative and formally renounced terrorism, recognising Israel and called for negotiations. On 15 November, Palestinian independence was declared. The Palestinians had gained a great deal of international sympathy during the *Intifada* but lost much of this moral advantage in August 1990 when the leadership and the majority of the people expressed their support for the Iraqi invasion of Kuwait. More seriously, financial support from conservative Arab countries was curtailed. The process of the disintegration of the Soviet Union, which was to collapse entirely in the last days of 1991, further increased the isolation of the Palestinians.

In this changing world, negotiations opened in Madrid in October 1991, involving Israelis, Palestinians, Jordanians, Syrians, and Lebanese meeting under American and Russian auspices. The talks had two parts: a series of bilateral talks between Israel and Syria, Lebanon, Jordan, and the Palestinians and multilateral talks on five functional issues: water, refugees, environment, economic development, and security. In 1992 Yitzhak Rabin became Prime Minister of Israel. In September 1993, he and Yasser Arafat met in Washington to sign a solemn declaration to end the conflict. Following a Declaration of Principles of 13 September 1993 and the Cairo Agreement of 4th of May 1994 in July 1994, the PLO was renamed the Palestinian Authority (PA).

In the years that followed, however, the peace negotiations have made little progress. Acts of violence against civilians, expansion of settlements, land confiscation, and collective punishments by the Israelis continued. In September 2000 Ariel Sharon lit the fuse that started the second *Intifada* when he entered the Haram (Temple Mount area) in Jerusalem, beginning a vicious cycle of violence that shows no signs of abatement. At the time of writing (December 2003) 2,580 Palestinian civilians have been killed in the course of the current uprising and 24,038 injured. 898 Israelis have been killed and 6,004 injured. 67 percent of Gaza Palestinians are unemployed and 48 percent in the West Bank.[45] 75 percent of Palestinians are now living below the official poverty level of less than $2 per day. The Palestinian Authority is boxed into a corner where it is unable to either negotiate or resist, and suicide bombers acting as desperate individuals or as agents of hard-line Palestinian groups have provoked still more draconian Israeli reprisals. At the time of writing there appears to be no movement in the situation other than an ever-increasing spiral of bloodshed and violence.

The common popular assumption that the conflict derives from religion can only be based on ignorance. Nevertheless, religious sentiment has become more and more of an incendiary factor in the clash of nationalisms. We have seen that both Zionism and the Palestinian national movement were primarily secular movements, but from their beginnings neither could entirely ignore the religious element in their construct of a national identity. In due course, religious fundamentalist groupings would come to constitute the most militant and intransigent supporters of the two respective nationalist ideologies. In the case of Zionism, the intrusion of religion as a major factor in nationalist ideology began after 1967. In the Palestinian case, however,

---

[45] Of this figure 266 of the dead were members of the Israeli Defense Forces and between 30 and 40 were Palestinian Israelis. 85 percent of Palestinian deaths were civilians with 19 percent under 18. Information from the Council for the Advancement of Arab-British Understanding, London (Intifada Facts Sheet, February 2003) and B'tselem (Israeli Information Center for Human Rights) http: //www.btselem.org.

militant Islam did not gain strength until after the defeat of the PLO in Lebanon in 1982.[46] In the case of Zionism, the biblical vision of the return to Zion was too deeply ingrained in Jewish culture to be ignored or left to the apolitically pious.[47] Likewise Palestinian Muslims could hardly avoid the appeal to religious solidarity from the Muslim world that saw the conflict in largely religious terms.[48]

Despite such manipulation of religious symbols and associations, the vast majority of religious Jews were opposed to Zionism right up until the events of 1967. However, the capture of the Old City of Jerusalem and the phenomenon of Israeli soldiers praying at the Western Wall touched upon Jewish religious sentiments in ways that the majority of religious Jews found hard to resist and which secular Zionists were only too eager to exploit.

In Israel today, as in the Jewish communities worldwide, religious Jews fall broadly into three categories. The first are the small number of Zionist religious Jews in the reform tradition[49] who try to accommodate religious sentiment with modernity and who tend, to be the most open to political compromise.[50]

After repeated denunciations of Zionism by the organisations of Reform Judaism, the period following the Balfour Declaration in 1917 saw a minority of Reform Jews who were more sympathetic to Zionism. In the

---

[46] B M Edwards, *Islamic Politics in Palestine,* Tauris, London, 1996, 8.

[47] Thus the Hebrew name given for the Jewish National Fund by the Zionist movement in 1901 was *Keren Kayemet L'Yisrael* which derived from liturgical terminology associated with the offering of 'first fruits' to God in the context of Exodus symbolism. This 'illustrates a secular manipulation of religious traditions' that 'evoked the foundational legend of deliverance from Egypt and entrance into the promised land.' Prior, *op. cit.,* 1999, 91.

[48] 'At a popular level, the conflict with Israel was usually interpreted in religious terms in Muslim countries outside the Arab world ...' Gee, *op. cit.,* 102.

[49] Reform Judaism was founded in 19th century Germany, becoming particularly prevalent in the United States, and was characterised from the beginning by universalism and the spirit of the Enlightenment from which it had grown.

[50] Their universalistic and liberal outlook was quite opposed to Zionist nationalism, regarding Jewish identity as religious rather than national. In response to Herzl's convening of the First Zionist Congress in 1897, the Central Conference of American Rabbis reaffirmed its opposition to Zionism by stating that, Judaism was 'not political nor national, but spiritual, and addresses itself to the continuous growth of peace, justice, and love in the human race, to a messianic time when all men will recognize that they form 'one great brotherhood' for the establishment of God's Kingdom on earth.' S Halperin, *The Political World of American Zionism,* Wayne State University Press, Detroit, Michigan, 1961, 72.

decades that followed, 'There were signs of a gradual conversion to Zionist values, seen firstly in support for the efforts of the labour movement in Palestine.'[51] Immigration of Jews from eastern European into the United States and the persecution of Jews under Hitler accelerated the pace of this conversion.[52] The establishment of the State of Israel and the events of 1967 were to leave the anti-Zionist adherents of Reform Judaism increasingly isolated and irrelevant.[53] Meanwhile, the alliance between observant religious Judaism also manifested itself in the influence of the religious political parties,[54] the incorporation of biblical motifs into national aetiological myths, and the handing over of matters matrimonial exclusively to the Orthodox Rabbinate.

The second grouping are those who belong to that Orthodox constituency who believe in a physical separation from mainstream Israeli society. These might typically be found in the Mea Shearim quarter of Jerusalem where the *haredi* and *Hasidim* live lives of strict piety in physical separation form mainstream Israeli society.[55] These religious Jews are typically either apolitical or, in some cases, anti-Zionist.[56] By comparison, there are

---

[51] Commenting on this conversion Louis Jacobs, 'Reformers do not see themselves as unprincipled in the change from opposition to acceptance of Zionism and Zionism's implications, since, on the reform view, it has always been the nature of Judaism to adapt itself to new ideas and new conditions of Jewish life.' L Jacobs, *op. cit.*, 416.

[52] Prior, *op. cit.*, 77-8.

[53] Despite this conversion, in Israel itself the reform movements in Judaism were granted no recognition and, although the new state was avowedly secular, a powerful alliance soon developed between observant Judaism and the new state. This resulted in the exclusion of Conservative, Liberal and Reformed Synagogue institutions from any role in Israeli public life.

[54] The Israeli voting system has the unintended effect of giving the small religious parties an influence out of all proportion to the number of votes they attract and enables them to 'trade' their support for minority governments in return for concessions giving an increasingly religious character to Israeli life. Financial subsidies for religious educational institutions, legislation on kosher food and the observance of the Sabbath, and the exclusion of non-Orthodox Jewish rabbis from national life are examples of ways in which this influence operates.

[55] Most of the inhabitants of Mea Shearim see the Jewish state as a blasphemy, as the Messiah has not yet arrived. M Reiss, 'Jewish Fundamentalism', *Holy Land Hollow Jubilee: God Justice and the Palestinians,* N Ateek and M Prior, eds., Melisende, London, 1999, 168-79.

[56] The suburb of *Mea Shearim* contains groupings of ultra-observant Jews characterised as much by their factional hostility to each other as to non-observant Jews. *Mea Shearim* was established for the 114 families from England, Germany, Austria, Russia, and Turkey in 1874 and was one of the first urban Jewish communities outside the Old City walls. The men often have the status of *talmidei hakhamim* (disciples of the learned and wise), which means that they devote their time exclusively to prayer and the study of sacred texts.

other strictly observant Jews such as the Lubavitchas[57] who stress meticulous piety and an indifference to politics but who are in principle allied to those with the uncompromising political attitudes towards any accommodation with the Palestinians.

Under the third heading are those religiously observant Jews who are quite active about their extreme nationalism. These religious Zionists see the Jewish State as part of the messianic plan and regard nationalism as the highest form of religious virtue. For them the Israeli victory in the Six Day War was miraculous, and territories restored to Israel by God may not be surrendered. They have been active in establishing illegal settlements in the West Bank and Gaza.

The most significant of these groups *Gush Emunim* (the Bloc of the Faithful) were foremost in the rank of religious Zionists to emerge after the Six Day War. *Gush Emunim* used civil disobedience to oppose Israeli withdrawal of the Sinai after the peace agreement in 1978 and threatened the same policy when the agreements of 1993 promised the return of some of the occupied territories to the Palestinians. A supporter of this tendency assassinated Yitzhak Rabin on November 1995.

However, if 1967 was a watershed in the relationship between Judaism and Zionism, the theological groundwork had already been done. Rabbi Avraham (Rav) Yitzhak Kook, the first Ashkenazi Chief Rabbi of Palestine (1921-35) had already produced the theoretical synthesis of Judaism and Zionism to which groups like the *Gush Emunim* could appeal.[58]

If Herzl was the chief architect of secular Zionism, Rabbi Kook (1865-1935) was the pioneer of the observant religious version, bringing together the religious longing for the spiritual symbol of Zion with the avowedly secular vision of building a Jewish state. Kook identified with the Revisionist Zionists[59] and characterised secular Zionists as unknowingly serving as God's instrument 'to further the messianic redemption and restoration

---

[57] The Lubavitch, a Hasidic group founded in Russia in the 18th century, regard the conversion of Jews to strict observance of the Law as a necessary prerequisite to the coming of the Messiah. L Cohn-Sherbok, 'Lubavi(t)ch,' John Bowker, ed., *The Oxford Dictionary of World Religions,* Oxford University Press, Oxford, 1997, 588.

[58] The influence of Rav Kook on Gush Emunim was mediated through the much more politicised ideas of his son Rabbi Zvi Yehuda Kook and his follower Israel Medad who regarded Palestinian Arabs as foreign occupiers and for whom 'the territory of *Eretz Israel* is assigned a sanctity which obligates its retention once liberated from foreign rule, as well as its settlement, even in defiance of government authority.' Gilbert, *op. cit.,* 469.

[59] When the revisionist Avraham Stavsky was accused of being implicated in the political assassination of the Labour Zionist Chaim Arlosoroff, Kook supported Stavsky and denounced the accusation as a 'blood libel' by Jews against a Jew. Gilbert, *op. cit.,* 72.

not only of Jews, but of all humanity'.[60] The redemption of the Land of Israel was to be seen as a prerequisite for the coming of the Messiah and for the Jewish people becoming the light to the nations.

Another example of the militant religious right in Israeli politics is represented by the *Kach* ('only thus') movement founded in 1972 by Rabbi Meir Kahane (1932-1990) on a platform of expelling all Arabs from Israel and the occupied territories and openly approving of the attacks on Palestinians. Elected to the Knesset in 1984, he was disqualified under a law introduced in 1988 that excluded supporters of openly racist programmes. In 1984, a terrorist settler group 'Terror Against Terror' was formed, widely suspected to be the armed wing of Kahane's movement. Kahane himself was assassinated in the United States in 1990, but his movement survives as the most extreme example of theocratic Zionism. For Kahane's followers secular Israeli democracy is as much the enemy as the Palestinian movement. In addition, neither Christians nor Muslims have any place in a Jewish state. As with racist and fascistic movements elsewhere, the success of this movement is not measurable as much by its small electoral influence as by the extent to which it articulates viewpoints shared by a wider band of public opinion.

The uncompromising mirror image of the religious right in Israeli politics emerged as the movement of radical political Islam, which became a major force among the Palestinian population in the Occupied Territories as late as the 1980s and 1990s. After the defeat of 1982 and the unsuccessful peace negotiations of the 1990s, more pragmatic Muslim supporters of the secular nationalist Palestinian movement found themselves flanked by the zealotry of Hamas and Islamic Jihad.

The earlier roots of these movements lay in the influence of the Muslim Brotherhood among Palestinian refugees in Gaza after 1948. The Brotherhood had originated in Egypt in the 1920s, and among its Palestinian activists in Gaza was Sheikh Ahmad Yassin who founded the Mujama (Islamic Congress). This movement provided community service and support among the refugees and campaigned against secular and modernising tendencies in Palestinian society.[61]

In the seventies the Mujama had the slogan, 'How can uncovered women and men with Beatles haircuts liberate our holy places?' At first

---

[60] Prior, *op. cit.*, 1999, 71.

[61] 'While outsiders and external forces perceive Hamas ideology as threatening and extremist, most Palestinians do not see it, or its call for Jihad as a threat but rather as representing the aspirations of many Palestinians for a return to Islam in their society.' Milton-Edwards, *op. cit.*, 111.

Islamicising movements of this type had no nationalist political programme and may even have been encouraged by the Israeli authorities as a rival focus to the PLO. Internationally, however, militant Islam was gaining credibility as a new radical political force, not least through the successful Islamic revolution in Iran in 1979. The defeat of the PLO in 1982 left a vacuum filled by grass-roots leadership and organisations during the first *Intifada*. In February 1988, in response to plans for a peace conference proposed by United States Assistant Under-Secretary of State, Richard Murphy, Sheikh Yassin founded the Movement of the Islamic Resistance (*Harakat al-Muqawama al-Islamiyya*) which soon became known as Hamas (based on the Hebrew acronym for the Arabic title).[62] Hamas identified its inheritance by revering the name of Sheikh Izz ad-Din al-Qassam, who died fighting the British under the banner of Islam in 1935. Rejecting any compromise with or concessions to the Jewish state, Hamas operated independently during the *Intifada* calling its own strike days and refusing to observe those called by groups claiming loyalty to the official leadership. By 1990, Hamas had emerged as the main opponent of the PLO, able to mount a serious challenge to nationalist hegemony in the Gaza Strip and the West Bank. This challenge has been directed also at the State of Israel.[63] Around the same time, another radical Islamic organisation was formed calling itself Islamic Jihad. Although Palestinian Muslims are all Sunni, Islamic Jihad openly acknowledged its debt to the Shi'ite Iranian Revolution and, unlike Hamas, placed violent struggle as a form of Jihad at the centre of its agenda.[64] This kind of militant Islam is in sharp contrast both with the political abstentionism of earlier Muslim revivalist groups and the moderate nationalist, but primarily spiritual, message of Sufi teachers such as Sidi Shaykh Muhammad al-Jamal ar-Rifa'i as-Shadhili.[65]

The fanatical intransigence of both Jewish and Muslim religious militants became apparent in a period where serious peace negotiations were in progress. In February 1994 Baruch Goldstein opened fire on the Muslim congregation at the Tomb of the Patriarchs in Hebron and killed twenty-seven worshippers. On April reprisal attacks by Hamas took the form

---

[62] Gilbert, *op. cit.*, 527-8.

[63] Milton Edwards, *op. cit.*, 9.

[64] 'Nor is Hamas ideology premised solely on political violence or the radical overthrow of the existing order, although political violence has been incorporated as a strategy of the organisation. (This approach is in direct contrast to Islamic Jihad which is premised upon political violence but justified in the guise of Jihad).' *Ibid.*, 183.

[65] Information from www.sufimaster.org. Shaykh Jamal, a senior official in the administration of Al-Aqsa is a leader of the Shadhiliyya Order, an international Sufi movement with a web site at www.napanet.net.

of a suicide bombing in Afula and Hadera in which a total of fourteen Israelis were killed. These were the first of many suicide bombings, which have continued regularly since that time and have had the effect of strengthening support for the most intransigent elements on the Israeli right.

Christians have adopted some quite different perspectives on the Israeli-Palestinian conflict, ranging from identification with one or other of the two contending parties through to relative indifference. Those Western Christians identifying more or less uncritically with the Israeli side of the conflict divide into two main categories. The first and the most extreme of these consists of Christian Zionists who regard the State of Israel as fulfilling biblical prophecy and consider that Christians owe a debt of loyalty and support for the most uncompromising and expansionist policies of the Israeli government.[66] Influenced by their literalistic interpretation of biblical prophecies, they maintain that the return of the Jews to Sion is a necessary prelude to the Second Coming of Christ. This movement which has its has its origins in millenarian Christian Zionism going back to 17th century England,[67] gained wider support, particularly in the United States, after the founding of the Jewish State in 1948. However, it was the capture of Jerusalem in 1967 that fired the apocalyptic imagination and led to the Christian Zionist revival of the 1970s.[68]

The second category consider that the terrible sufferings which the Nazis inflicted on the Jews during the Second World War gives them a moral right to a state of their own. They also consider that the crimes committed against the Jews by Christians of past generations need to be compensated for by giving strong support for a secure Jewish homeland.

Those Christians who are critical of Israel and who identify with the Palestinian case see the Palestinians as the innocent victims of the

---

[66] Beliefs of Christian Zionists can be summarised as follows. Biblical prophecies are literal and predictive. The true Church will enjoy rapture into heaven, and Israel will become God's primary instrument. There are seven epochs or dispensations in human history. There is a dispensation of grace before the Millennium. The coming 'Tribulation', the battle of Armageddon, and the Second Coming of Christ are all events for which Christians must try to discern the signs. D Wagner, 'Reagan and Begin, Bibi and Jerry: The Theopolitical Alliance of the Likud Party with the American Christian Right',199-215, cited in N Ateek and M Prior, *Holy Land: Hollow Jubilee,* Melisende, London, 1998, xiv.

[67] This revival gained its strength from the influence of the tele-evangelists, the emergence of the 'Moral Majority' right-wing Christian fundamentalist movement, and the Christian Broadcasting Network. See D Wagner, 'Anxious for Armageddon; Probing Israel's Support among American Fundamentalists', H Haddad and D Wagner, eds., *All in the Name of the Bible,* Amana Books, Brattelboro, Vermont, 1986, 201-2.

[68] *Ibid.,* 23-4.

setting up of the State of Israel and emphasise that a small but important section of the Palestinian people is Christian. The Vatican and the Anglican Communion, in particular, are concerned about the continuation of an indigenous Christian presence in the Holy Land. They are also anxious that Jerusalem should not be in the hands of followers of just one of the three faiths for which it is holy.

Palestinian Christians themselves have generally supported the moderate nationalist camp and have rejected the infusion of religious zeal into political fanaticism, many of them advocating non-violent resistance to the occupation. They are conscious that they have shared in the sufferings inflicted on the Palestinian people as a whole and that many of their number have left the country to escape from situations of conflict and discrimination. Their leaders try to draw attention to the implications for the Christian world of the gradual disappearance of communities that have maintained a continuous presence in the Holy Land since Pentecost.

Other Christians have more nuanced approaches supporting the existence of the State of Israel but being critical of oppressive Israeli government policies.[69] The main criteria governing the attitudes to the conflict by Christianity at the official level have been concern for the safety of the holy places and the preservation of free access to them, the protection and survival of the indigenous Christians, and more general considerations of peace and justice.[70] Since 1948, there has also been concern by some to support the existence and safety of Israel as a way of atoning for past Christian crimes against the Jews. From this perspective, 'Disregard for Israel's safety and welfare is incompatible with the Church's necessary concern for the Jewish people.'[71] Inter-faith relations between Christians and Jews clearly have considerable influence upon attitudes to the conflict, but there is an

---

[69] See, for example, the Vatican statement recognising the 'the rights and legitimate aspirations of the Jews to a sovereign and independent state' balanced by a demand that there should be a reciprocal recognition of 'the rights and legitimate aspirations of another people, which have also suffered for a long time, the Palestinian people.' *Acta Apostolicae Sedis*, January–March 1976, 134.

[70] In his audience with American Jewish Committee leaders in February 1985, Pope John Paul II expressed the hope that 'The Lord give to the land, and to all the peoples and nations in that part of the world, the blessings contained in the word *shalom*' and 'that the sons and daughters of Abraham—Jews, Christians and Muslims—may live and prosper in peace.' M H Tanenbaum, 'A Jewish Viewpoint on Nostra Aetate', E J Fisher, A J Rudin and M H Tanenbaum, ed., *Twenty Years of Jewish Catholic Relations*, Paulist Press, Maywah, New York, 1986, 58-9.

[71] *A New Way of Thinking. Guidelines for the Churches*, Commission for Inter-Faith Relations: Christians and Jews, Council of Churches for Britain and Ireland, London, 1994, 14.

increasing realisation that this needs to be balanced by a parallel concern to promote good relations between Christians and Muslims.[72]

From a Christian point of view it is also important to retain a sense of theological perspective. Contemporary preachers are rightly warned against interpreting the New Testament in ways that are detrimental to Jewish Christian relations or supportive of anti-semitic ideologies. From this unexceptionable perspective, however, some writers wish to go further and talk as though there was no sense in which Christ fulfils the earlier Covenant.[73]

From this distorted theological perspective in which Judaism and Christianity are seen as parallel covenants with equivalent value, the political perspective of Christian Zionism follows easily. If Christ does not fulfil the Law and the Prophets, the modern State of Israel emerges as an alternative candidate. There is a danger in giving a nation-state the status of being divinely promised. Politics is a grubby business, and any state is liable to be involved in oppression towards the defenceless, aggressive policies towards its neighbours, espionage, wars and deceit. In the case of Israel, many would regard the negative case as overwhelming. Unless or until some measure of justice is achieved for those who have endured the evils of displacement, exile, and military occupation, Israel should be one of the last states to have its nationalism validated by Christian preachers. For Christian critics of Zionism, the acceptance of Zionism involves collusion with the injustice done to the Palestinians.[74] Meanwhile, for some religious Jews the granting of messianic status to the State of Israel is not only dangerous but also blasphemous.[75]

The impact of the Liberation Theology perspective that emerged primarily out of Latin America in the 1960s and 70s has obvious relevance to the Israeli-Palestinian conflict. The fundamental tenets of Liberation

---

[72] An account of the influence of conflicting demands of inter-faith dialogue is to be found in Chapter V: 'Multi Faith Pluralism and Preaching in a Holy Land Perspective.'

[73] For example, J Pawlikowski, 'Ethical Issues in the Israeli Palestinian Conflict', in R Reuther and M Ellis, eds., *Beyond Occupation: American Jews, Christians and Palestinians*, Beacon Press, Boston, 1990, 155-70, or P van Buren, *Discerning the Way: A Theology of Jewish Christian Reality*, Seabury, New York, 1980. In a debate with Messianic Christian theologian David Stern, Friedrich-Wilhelm Marquardt argues that traditional christological doctrines must be rejected. Stern counters this by asserting that Jesus must continue to be regarded as the Messiah both of the Jews and of the gentiles. H Hegstad, 'Saviour of the Gentiles or Israel's Messiah?', *Theology Digest*, Summer 1997, 112.

[74] Prior, *op. cit.*, 1999, 147-52.

[75] *Ibid.*, 227-9.

Theology are those of the 'preferential option for the poor'[76] and 'praxis'[77]—breaking down the distinction between abstract theory and its practical application. Both these tenets have as their premise the recovery of the communal dimension of Christianity, rejecting preoccupation with 'soul saving' individualism that does not also embrace the imperatives of affirming bodily and material needs, and the liberation of communities experiencing exploitation and oppression. The application of these principles clearly invites an active concern for the plight of the Palestinians—Muslim and Christian alike. It also provides a commitment that transcends the limitations of nationalist ideology. Rather, it looks beyond the redressing of an historic injustice towards a liberation that includes all the parties to the present conflict. In the words of Naim Ateek, the pioneer of a Palestinian Liberation Theology, 'when the oppressed are set free, their dignity and humanity is restored to them and they become free human beings. When the land is returned to its legal owners, it means that people can cultivate it and live from the gift of the land and the produce which God has given them. When the debt of the poor is cancelled they can have a fresh start with hope for a better future for themselves and their families. The jubilee allows for new attitudes to develop and new perceptions to be created. The Palestinians and Israelis will not perceive each other as enemies, but as potential friends and partners.'[78]

Preaching Plan: Isaiah 61: 1-6 and Luke 4: 14-30[79]
Preparation of the Homily: Process and Strategies

This preaching plan is for a homily on the preaching of Jesus at the synagogue in Nazareth as recorded in Luke 4. It was given at the evening service at the

---

[76] 'Jesus, like the prophets, concentrates on those areas where the life of individuals is most precarious, most threatened, or even non-existent. For this reason the program of his mission is one of partiality and announces a God of partisan life to those who lack it at the most elementary levels.' John Sobrino, *Jesus in Latin America,* Orbis, Maryknoll, New York, 1987, 107-8.

[77] 'Existing liberation theology is a theology directed upon praxis—precisely a praxis of social transformation ... at once critical and utopian.' C Boff, 'Epistemology and Methodology of the Theology of Liberation', I Ellacuria and J Sobrino, eds., *Mysterium Liberationis. Fundamental Concepts of Liberation Theology,* Orbis, Maryknoll, New York, 1993, 65.

[78] N Ateek, 'Preface,' in N Ateek and M Prior, *op. cit.,* xiv.

[79] When he came to Nazareth, where he had been brought up, he went to the synagogue on the Sabbath day, as was his custom. He stood up to read, and the scroll of the prophet Isaiah

United Reformed Church in Twickenham and was preached from the perspective of a reminiscence of preaching at Nazareth after time in Jerusalem and the West Bank and a journey to Jericho and up the Jordan Valley to Nazareth. The preaching reflects upon the experience of visiting Yad Va Shem, contemplating the Jewish story of tragedy and homecoming and sets this beside the Palestinian story, attempting to situate both narratives within the context of the 'preaching of good news for the poor' and a freedom for captives' as preached by Jesus.

Preparatory reading of commentary on this passage gave a strong sense of the importance of this passage for the whole of the subsequent narrative of Luke's Gospel. Whereas the other synopticists placed this incident on in the course of Jesus' ministry, Luke places it at the beginning and 'transforms the account by the addition of the citation from Isaiah and the speech of Jesus. The passage is made into a programmatic prophecy which guides the readers understanding of the subsequent narrative.'[80] From a narrowly historical critical perspective, however, programmatic prophecy involved in Jesus' use of Isaiah's language of liberation is not necessarily seen as applicable to the political or economic realms.[81]

---

was given to him. He unrolled the scroll and found the place where it was written: 'The Spirit of the Lord is upon me, because he has anointed me to bring good news to the poor. He has sent me to proclaim release to the captives and recovery of sight to the blind, to let the oppressed go free, to proclaim the year of the Lord's favour.' And he rolled up the scroll, gave it back to the attendant, and sat down. The eyes of all in the synagogue were fixed on him. Then he began to say to them, 'Today this scripture has been fulfilled in your hearing.' (Luke 4: 14-30)

All spoke well of him and were amazed at the gracious words that came from his mouth. They said, 'Is not this Joseph's son?' 'He said to them, 'Doubtless you will quote to me this proverb, "Doctor, cure yourself!" And you will say, "Do here also in your hometown the things that we have heard you did at Capernaum."' And he said, 'Truly I tell you, no prophet is accepted in the prophet's hometown. But the truth is, there were many widows in Israel in the time of Elijah, when the heaven was shut up three years and six months, and there was a severe famine over all the land; yet Elijah was sent to none of them except to a widow at Zarephath in Sidon. There were also many lepers in Israel in the time of the prophet Elisha, and none of them was cleansed except Naaman the Syrian.' When they heard this, all in the synagogue were filled with rage. They got up, drove him out of the town, and led him to the brow of the hill on which their town was built, so that they might hurl him off the cliff. But he passed through the midst of them and went on his way.

[80] Johnson, *op. cit.,* 82.

[81] Johnson recognizes the possibility that the words as used by Jesus can be seen as referring to 'the eschatological Jubilee year, when all debts would be remitted and slaves manumitted (Lev 25: 10-18)' but considers that 'rather than picturing Jesus' work in terms of political or economic reform, Luke portrays his liberating work in terms of personal exorcisms, healings and the teachings of the people.' *Ibid.,* 91.

Nor is there any shortage of non-political hermeneutic for this passage in the writings of the Fathers. Origen considers that 'by 'the poor' he means the gentile nations,' and Cyril of Jerusalem sees the recipients of the good news as 'the poor in spirit'.[82] Seeking to identify the captives who are to be set free, John Chrysostom, at his most patriarchal and least golden mouthed, cites 2 Timothy 3: 6 ('leading captive silly women laden with sins') for an example of moral and spiritual captivity. For Chrysostom, however, 'The worst captivity is of the mind ... for sin exercises the worst of all tyrannies, commanding to do evil and destroying them that obey it. From this prison of the soul Christ sets us free.'[83]

For a meeting of sound historical critical exegesis with a contemporary liberationist hermeneutic, Michael Prior's *Jesus the Liberator* offers a rigorous analysis of the verses in question, from every critical and sociological perspective, before producing a contemporary reading for today. In his conclusion he insists that, 'the Christian Church, if it is to be faithful to its founder from Nazareth, should be at the forefront of transformation, not only by offering the world the liberation rhetoric of Lk. 4: 16-30, but by contributing to goals and strategies by which the poor can experience the blessedness of the gospel.'[84]

The universalism of Jesus' message is underlined by the fact that the reference to the story of the widow in 1 Kings 17: 1-16 is described as living in Zarephath, modern Sarepta 'located near Sidon on the Phoenician coast, making the woman a gentile.'[85] Likewise, Naaman the Syrian from the story in 2 Kings 5: 1-14 is a gentile. It is this universalism that offends the congregation. 'What makes all of this preaching so unacceptable is that the people of Jesus' time expected Messiah to come and destroy Israel's enemies not to minister to them.'[86] Again, 'It is this veiled intimation that the prophet would be for all and not just for them—and in the reader's understanding, that God's visitation and salvation were to be for the poor and the oppressed of all nations and not just for the Jews—that arouses the neighbors' wrath,

---

[82] John H Newman, *Catena Aurea (Commentary on the Four Gospels Collected Out of the Works of the Fathers by Saint Thomas Aquinas, Volume Three: St Luke, first published in English in 1941)*, The Saint Austin Press, Southampton, 1997, 155.

[83] 156.

[84] M Prior, *Jesus the Liberator: Nazareth Liberation Theology (Luke 4. 16-30)*, Sheffield Academic Press, Sheffield, 1995, 200.

[85] Johnson, *op. cit.*, 80.

[86] C A Evans, 'Third Sunday after Epiphany, Year C', R van Harn, ed., *The Lectionary Commentary, Theological Exegesis of Sunday's Texts, The Third readings: the Gospels,* Eerdmans, Grand Rapids, Michigan, 2001, 326.

impelling them to fulfill Jesus' statement: he is not acceptable in his own country because his mission extends beyond his own country.'[87]

This insight is given contemporary application in Prior's study and gives examples of contextualised theologies in South Africa, Brazil, and Palestine. In Prior's words, 'The circumstances of the indigenous Christian communities are ripe for theological reflection on life under military occupation within the Occupied Territories and on life as third, fourth or fifth class citizens of the Jewish State of Israel.'[88] The homily that follows derives from just such reflection.

Text of Homily

PROBLEMATIC

These words present a powerful picture of human liberation. They constitute a manifesto of freedom for captives and an end to poverty and oppression. I want you to imagine that you are hearing these words in Nazareth. We are on a pilgrimage to the Holy Land and we are now in the town where Luke tells us that Jesus preached on this text from Isaiah at the Sabbath service in the synagogue at the start of his ministry. Like many pilgrims we have come to Nazareth after some days in Jerusalem and the territories. There we have been visiting places associated with the Gospel story. But we have also been conscious of two other stories—the stories of two people, the Israelis and the Palestinians. And today we have some difficulty trying to connect these two stories not only with each other but also with the message of Jesus in the synagogue in Nazareth.

One story was the story of the Jewish people and their return to Zion after centuries of captivity and oppression. The other story we have brought with us to Nazareth is the story of the Palestinian people, still enduring dispossession, captivity, and oppression.

One way out of this dilemma—of which story to relate to the words quoted by Jesus—might be to say that the test from Isaiah, now in the mouth of Jesus, is general and inclusive. The words can and perhaps should be interpreted in a spiritual sense. They are about the preaching of the good news to the spiritually impoverished, to those who are blind to God's love, to those who are in bondage to sin. But any interpretation of these words that does not connect them with political realities is not being true either to their original meaning in Isaiah or to Christian Faith in the Incarnation.

It is not true to the original meaning of Isaiah from the time after the return of the exiles from Babylon. They had returned, but their oppression had not ended. This section of Isaiah[89] draws on the figure of the servant found in an earlier section,[90] written

---

[87] Johnson, *op. cit.*, 82.

[88] M Prior, *op. cit.*, 1995, 189.

[89] Chapters 56-66, often called 'Trito-Isaiah'.

[90] Chapters 40-55, known as 'Deutro-Isaiah'.

two generations before. The servant would liberate the captives. The original sense was profoundly political.

It is not true to Christian Faith in the Incarnation, because in Christ God became fully human—with a human body as well as a human soul. Any interpretation of the New Testament that does not speak to the bread and butter concerns of our times is not true to that insight.

THE ISRAELI STORY

Like many Christian pilgrims coming to Nazareth from Jerusalem, we have visited YadVaShem and followed the dreadful story of the Nazi genocide of the Jews. We may have been moved by different things: by the art museum with its paintings and drawings, by concentration camp prisoners, by the collection of teddies and other toys once belonging to the children, by the hall of names recording the names of over three million victims. For me, the most moving place in YadVaShem was the Childrens' Memorial, designed by an architect whose own son was murdered in Auschwitz at the age of two and a half. You stand there in the darkness and you hear the recitation of the names and ages of an endless litany of names and ages of slaughtered innocents. So moving is the story of the sufferings of the Jews in Europe that we long to make it a story not of heart-numbing evil but of redemption and hope. Surely, we want to say the establishment of the State of Israel in 1948 can provide just such a happy ending.

THE PALESTINIAN STORY

But happy ending for one people—if that is what it was—was not the happy ending for another. During our time in Jerusalem we only needed to have gone as far as Bethlehem to have seen the roadblocks and the queues of people at the road blocks. If we had only gone as far as Bethlehem we would have seen the shell holes and the damaged buildings, the pain and resentment in the eyes of a people that have been deprived of dignity and hope. If we went as far as Gaza, we would have seen the fetid slums of the most overcrowded place in the world. Lastly, on the way through the Jordan Valley we saw the ruins of the three refugee camps outside Jericho. Here in 1948, 185,000 Palestinian refugees made their homes until, in 1967, most of them left for new camps in Jordan.[91] YadVaShem itself is built on land seized from Christian Palestinians in 1948.[92]

---

[91] In June 1967, in the days immediately following the Six Day War, the Israeli authorities organised the transfer of 200,000 Palestinians from the West Bank. These included 100,000 inhabitants of the refugee camps near Jericho. See Masalha, 1997, 84-8.

[92] YadVaShem is built on land belonging to the village of Ein Karem, the traditional birthplace of John the Baptist. In July 1948, a population of 4,500 mainly Catholic Christian Palestinians was forced to leave by the Jewish militia. It is one of the major ironies of history that the YadVaShem, a memorial to the Jewish victims of the Nazis, is built on the terraced land of the dispossessed, exiled, and involuntarily 'absentee' Palestinians of Ein Karem. Information supplied by website at http://www.sabeel.org/news/newslt15/matar.html.

The Palestinians, Christian and Muslim alike, are still waiting for their happy ending; for the word of freedom for prisonesr, for the setting free of the oppressed.

GOOD NEWS

But the good news preached by a message is a declaration of something that is real: 'This text is fulfilled today even as you are listening.' The coming of Jesus the anointed one is the fulfilment of the promise. It is for us to take up the challenge of the fulfilment of that promise. It is for us to apply it at every level—both at the personal level and at the political level, too. And at every level we note that it is inclusive and never narrowly nationalistic. When the people of Nazareth doubted him, he reminded them that Elijah healed a widow of Zarephat rather than any of the widows in Israel, that he cured Naaman the Syrian rather than any of the lepers of Israel.

APPLICATION

It is understandable that so many people have welcomed the setting up of a Jewish state as a sign of liberty to captives, as a setting free of a people who endured so much. Historically, however, the injustice of losing their homes suffered by the Palestinians was something planned and intended by at least some of the leaders of the Zionist movement from the beginning, long before the Nazi genocide. And from the perspective of the preaching of Jesus, liberation is always more than national liberation. It must be based on God's justice and must embrace people of all nationalities. 'There were many widows in Israel … but Elijah was not sent to one of these … . And in the prophet Elisha's time there were many lepers in Israel but none of these was cured—only Naaman the Syrian.'

It seems to me to be obvious that the Palestinians, like all oppressed people everywhere, have a right to the active support of those who follow the teaching of Jesus. To decide who is oppressed and who is the oppressor requires that we should do our homework and look in detail at matters over which people disagree. However, we cannot duck the issue. Sometimes it involves the recognition that the same party that is captive and oppressed in one situation is the oppressor and the gaoler in another. The word of freedom spoken by Jesus is a word that lightens our hearts and sets us frees. It is our task to make sure that the same word is spoken to all and that their freedom is assured.

Chapter 7
PILGRIMAGE REMEMBERED AND PILGRIMAGE IMAGINED

Sion shall be called 'Mother' for all will be her children (Psalm 87 [86]: 5) [G].

The word of freedom spoken by Jesus may indeed be a word intended to lighten hearts and set the downtrodden free. However, the task of passing on that word and of releasing its liberating power falls to human preachers who are obliged to draw not only from the wealth of Scripture and Tradition but also from their own experiences and homiletic skills. The final section of this book offer a summary of the results of surveys providing empirical evidence that examined the relevance of the preacher's experience of the Holy Land and evaluated responses to preaching that consciously draw from that experience.[1]

The first element of enquiry involved evaluation of the experience of 'preacher pilgrims,' ministers of the Word who had visited the Holy Land, seeking to identify the relevance of such visits to the development of the pilgrim-preacher's homiletic range. The second element comprises the responses of 'Partners in Preaching' focus groups to four of the homilies included in this volume. It then provided an account of a 'Virtual Pilgrimage' given for the Catholic Chaplaincy at Iowa State University in January 2003 and summarised responses from a focus group asked to evaluate the preaching. In the conclusion, there was a summary of issues that had been identified and of questions still outstanding. These will be seen to support the argument that the perspective offered by the Holy Land can and should contribute to the devotional and preaching imagination of the wider Church.

The first batch of 'preacher-pilgrims' was drawn from Faculty and Doctor of Ministry in Preaching students at Aquinas Institute of Theology in St Louis, Missouri.[2] One might expect some differences of outlook and expectations between a predominantly American multi-denominational

---

[1] The full account of the questionnaires and surveys referred to here is published in full in my thesis written in partial fulfilment of the requirements for the Doctor of Ministry in Preaching, 'Preaching and the Holy Land', 2003. The thesis is available in the library of the Aquinas Institute at St Louis, Missouri and as an attachment link to the publications page on www.deaconduncan.com

[2] This was done through the good offices of Fisher's Net, a provider of online theological post-graduate courses in the United States.

sample and those of a British/Irish-British group in which most of the participants were Roman Catholic priests. To test this assumption I based the second study upon the experiences of members of the Upper Thames Deanery in the Archdiocese of Westminster. The normal monthly meeting of the Deanery doubled as a focus group, and its findings were supplemented by a questionnaire completed by absentees and by participants who left before the meeting the meeting ended. Those responding to the questionnaires or participating in the focus groups were all people who had experienced pilgrimage to the Holy Land, either as leaders or as participants.

In view of the security situation in the Holy Land, there was no reason to suppose that either of these first two groups had any very recent experience of being in the Holy Land. Nor did I expect that members of either group would have gone there with any specific political commitment. For this reason, I decided that the next group studied should be composed of experienced pilgrims and pilgrim group leaders who had visited the Holy Land during the last three years and who had an acknowledged commitment to one side or the other in the Israeli-Palestinian conflict. The sample chosen was made up of those present at a committee of the British branch of the 'Friends of *Sabeel*,' an organisation supporting an ecumenical Palestinian Liberation Theology project in Jerusalem. This focus group was allowed a free ranging discussion that covered not only the experience of pilgrimage for members of the group but also the aims and objectives of *Sabeel* pilgrimage organisers.

The fourth study in this group is an interview with Lucy Winkett, Canon Precentor of St Paul's Cathedral, spokesperson for a very recently returned fact-finding mission to the Holy Land organised for a group of Anglican and Methodist women ministers in 2002. This experience was particularly interesting, as the group had no previous experience of pilgrimage to the Holy Land and no particular political preconceptions. They had also been exposed to the experiences of both Israelis and Palestinians. The fact that they were all women preachers added an additional dimension to the experience.

The second element of empirical enquiry gathers responses to four of the homilies included in this work via the medium of focus group discussions. The first homily on the Epiphany was preached at a Sunday Mass at Our Lady of Light Catholic Church in Clacton on Sea, Essex. The second homily, on the Gadarene Swine, was preached to a small congregation at a weekday Mass during an optional seminar for Doctor of Ministry in Preaching students in Venice, Florida. The remaining two homilies were given at the United Reformed Church in Twickenham. One of these was on the

Samaritan woman at the well (John 4), and the other was on the preaching of Jesus at Nazareth, Luke 4: 18-30.

For the virtual pilgrimage to the Holy Land, two schemas were devised for preached pilgrimage itineraries. These might have been suitable either for actual pilgrimage to the Holy Land or for 'virtual pilgrimage.' Virtual pilgrimage is appropriate for groups of people who are either unable to visit the Holy Land or unwilling to take the risk of doing so in a period of military conflict and the threat of a regional war. The pilgrimage of the imagination outlined here was in fact preached in December 2002 for the Catholic Chaplaincy at Iowa State University.

Preacher pilgrims

The questionnaire used in the survey conducted online through the good offices of Fisher's Net, a ministry of the Evangelical Lutheran Church in America, and also given to the Upper Thames Deanery was the same in each case.[3]

Members of the Upper Thames Deanery were asked the same questions as the Fisher's Net group and those individuals unable to participate in the discussion or obliged to leave before the end had the opportunity to send in the written responses included in the table that followed. Written responses by two other priests from the diocese were also included in order to enlarge the sample. An account of the focus group discussion was provided first, together with an analysis comparing the responses of this group with the Fisher's Net responses.

The discussion by a group at the deanery meeting was recorded and is summarised here. Nineteen people were present, including two deacons, two religious sisters, and a female lay religious education co-ordinator. Of these, six had not been to the Holy Land but remained present for the discussion.

The discussion showed a marked similarity in the experiences of the individuals in the group and a considerable consensus in the views expressed. All of those who had been to the Holy Land had been with groups once or several times. Half had stayed in Arab hotels or Church hospices and half in Israeli hotels. Most had experienced Israeli guides and only just over a third had met and worshipped with Palestinian Christians.

---

[3] http//fishersnet.blackboard.com.webpapps./assessment/take.jsp?course_assessment_id=...
   1/29/03.

All of them considered that the experience of the Holy Land had enhanced their preaching—particularly at the level of 'bringing the Scriptures alive'. Lacking a Liberation Theology perspective, only a few mentioned the impact that their experience in the Holy Land might have had upon their preaching on peace and justice issues. Insights into inter-faith dialogue were included in a few cases, and most of these were in relation to Jewish-Christian rather than Muslim-Christian relations. Several people said that their perceived experience of the Israelis had made Jewish-Christian dialogue appear more difficult.

After a number of similar expressions of opinion on the Israeli-Palestinian conflict a show of hands was invited, and it transpired that although about a third of the group acknowledged going out with pro-Israeli prejudices every single member of the group came back with pro-Palestinian sympathies. It should perhaps be pointed out that one member of the group had visited the Holy Land as a guest of the Israeli Tourist Board. The current situation evinced a number of comments reflecting pessimism and dismay.

Comparisons between responses of this group with the largely American Fisher's Net group showed considerable overlap. However, the American group was seen to have had less opportunity to meet with or worship with Palestinian Christians and to be less likely to have developed insights or appreciation of Islam. Indeed, inter-faith relations in general seemed to figure as a more unfamiliar concept to American respondents. Also, fewer saw any application of the lessons of the Israeli-Palestinian conflict to political repression worldwide.

In general, the British group was more wholeheartedly pro-Palestinian and the American groups seemed less likely to express a political opinion. This might have reflected the influence of a more emphatically pro-Israeli media in the United States, or it might have been affected by the closer links between Israeli and American travel companies with a consequently wider use of Israeli travel facilities. Whichever influences may have been operative, however, it is remarkable that nobody in either group admitted to being strongly partisan on behalf of Israel. Among those who did attempt to analyse the issues of violence and justice, comments from the American group showed a tendency in some cases to moralise in an 'even-handed' way so as to excuse the respondent from specific political choices. The attitudes of the recorded discussion in the Upper Thames group were largely replicated in the written responses that followed.

Sabeel Focus Group

The 'Friends of *Sabeel*' focus group took place at a regular Friends of Sabeel committee meeting and provided the opportunity to discuss some of the same issues with a small group of politically committed Christians. In most cases members of this group had had considerable experience of participating, leading, and planning pilgrimages and of using their experience in their preaching. On the advice of the secretary of the group, no questionnaires were distributed. The discussion was loosely structured around two central areas: each individual member's account of his or her own 'conscientisation' over the issue of Palestinian rights and the impact of the experience of the Holy Land on their preaching.

Chairing the discussion myself, I began by asking each member of the group to address the question: 'Did your commitment to the cause of Palestinian rights arise directly from a visit to the Holy Land?' Answers indicated that their commitment had in most cases developed as process rather than as a Damascene conversion. For all but one the commitment had also been determined by a number of influences of which the experience of the land itself had had an important role to play.

T, an Anglican priest and retired aid worker, identified three stages in the development of his own thinking. Firstly, there was the question of geography. A visit to Jericho had brought home to him the importance of geography to biblical studies. He had already come to realise the wider importance of geography in providing the context for a Christian commitment to work for international justice and service of the poor. This realisation was vital to his professional work as part of a team involved in the issue of development in poorer countries. The second stage had been the influence of Jewish and Palestinian Christian thinkers. T had already read some of the work of Marc Ellis, with its advocacy of a Jewish Liberation Theology that takes seriously the rights of Palestinians. On a visit to the Holy Land he had also been exposed to the influence of Canon Naim Ateek and Rabbi Jeremy Milgrom, spokesperson for the group 'Rabbis for Human Rights.' The third stage had been the experience of a visit to Ein Karem. There he had been moved to tears by the sight of the houses formerly occupied by the Christian Palestinians driven out of their homes in 1948. When he had asked a Franciscan priest at the Church of the Visitation whether the words of the *Magnificat* might have any relevance for this historic injustice the priest was unable to relate his faith to this modern tragedy in any way.

Other members of the group spoke of the influence of individuals on their commitment to Palestinian rights, and the names of Naim Ateek and Marc Ellis recurred several times. W, a Methodist lay woman preacher, spoke of the disappointment experienced during her first pilgrimage at the way in which the guides and leaders of her group had refused to talk about the realities before their eyes. Eventually, helped by hearing Naim Ateek, she had been able to make the link between the Bible story and the contemporary political narrative in the Holy Land.

N, an Anglican priest, exceptionally for this group, had never been to the Holy Land but regarded his commitment to the Palestinians as integral to his passion for justice worldwide. The proper context of Christian theology and preaching was always to be found in contemporary issues.

M, a Catholic priest and academic, described how when he had gone to the Holy Land he had been moved by the plight of the Palestinians. He had discovered that the biblical context of his studies was also the context of the oppressor's own understanding. He had become concerned that the Bible narrative was too often interpreted as validating oppression. In his opinion the linkage between religion and violence needed to be 'pulled limb from limb.' Biblical readings that justified violence were read aloud in Church and the reader announced, 'This is the Word of God.' Questions about the nature of biblical inspiration needed to be examined. He had come to see the Jewish-Christian dialogue as having been corrupted by a Zionist agenda, and in turn it had exercised a corrupting influence itself in relation to political justice.

On the influence of the Holy Land on preaching, D, a former employee of *Sabeel* in Jerusalem, considered it important that the preacher should be able to make the linkage between the Bible and contemporary events in Palestine and elsewhere.

L, a Free Church minister, argued the need for contextual preaching with the power to 'turn our lives upside down.' Exposure to the Holy Land could help in this process but there was a danger of a 'little knowledge being a dangerous thing. Exposure to the Holy Land experience needed to be provided in generous quantities.

M reiterated that relating the Holy Land to preaching raised problematic questions about authority of the Bible. Preachers could appeal to the Bible and relate it to the Holy Land either to impart information or to confirm their own prejudices. He did sometimes relate the text to the conflict in the Holy Land but was anxious that he should not be dismissed as overly partisan in his opinions.

O, a veteran lay activist on Palestinian issues who had first visited the Holy Land in 1946, spoke eloquently from her own experience about the risk of losing friends by speaking the truth of what one had seen.

T spoke of how, in his preaching he had found that Israel-Palestine linked up with other global issues. On a pilgrimage in 1996, he had travelled from the Sea of Galilee down the Great Rift Valley and had reflected on the significance attached to the fact that the ministry of Jesus had been 'at the crossroads of the world'. 'God had known what he was doing' in making Palestine the theatre of the Incarnation. What happened in this place had a 'handle on history' everywhere.

Asked about the ecumenical dimension of the work of *Sabeel*, there was general agreement with the statement that the soundest basis for Christian unity is to be found in 'working together for justice and peace.'

Palestinian pilgrimage

Interview with Canon Lucy Winkett of St Paul's Cathedral after leading a pilgrimage of women clergy organised by Christian Aid early in 2003

Can you please tell me about the circumstances of the pilgrimage and what persuaded you to join it?
The invitation came originally from Christian Aid. Garth Hewitt asked me if I wanted to go out on a fact-finding trip for Christian Aid to one of the countries where Christian Aid works. I have preached regularly for Christian Aid and that I think that that was why he approached me. Originally it was not going to be the Holy Land but some other country, possibly the Philippines. Then he asked me how I felt about going as part of a women's group to the Middle East. I liked the fact that we were going as a group of women ministers because I thought it might be interesting to see how we reacted, as a group of women, to the context as well as how the context reacted to us as a group of women priests. I had never been on a classic pilgrimage to the Holy Land and hadn't really wanted to go on one but this seemed to be a great opportunity to go and to see—to coin a phrase—the Living Stones rather than just the buildings. That is how it came about. So we advertised that for a group of six or seven women ministers to fit in one minibus!

Where did you stay?
We stayed in St George's in Jerusalem for three days, in a hotel in Gaza City for three days and at then at the St Margaret's in Nazareth.

You have already said something about this on the Christian Aid video but can you think of ways in which your visit might have affected—or might in the future— affect the content of your preaching?

Quite a lot! The way that I have described it is that the words—the names of the towns—like Bethlehem and Nazareth—now mean something different for me. Bethlehem means water tanks with bullet holes in them as much as it means 'While shepherds watched their flocks by night.' It has changed the meaning of the places for me—very much so—and I think that that is particularly so around Christmas and Easter. I preached quite soon afterwards on the visit of Nicodemus to Jesus and I was much more aware of the context of military occupation as experienced by Palestinians today. So I found myself preaching about Nicodemus visiting Jesus by night as a meeting of two people under occupation. Nicodemus was talking to a radical and controversial figure and there was always the threat of violence by the authorities. I had not really thought much about that before.

The visit directly affected my preaching. When I was studying to be ordained I did a course on the Holocaust. I was interested in the Middle East anyway and the visit to the Holy Land helped me to understand the Palestinian perspective. I had studied the Holocaust and Jewish studies and with Christianity's roots being very much in Judaism I suppose I had automatically concentrated on the Jewish narrative.

Did you go to Yad VaShem?

Yes. We went to Yad VaShem. It was a very, very moving experience, particularly because a Jewish guide who worked in Christian-Jewish education took us round. He was very effective and somehow the stories were etched on his face.

Who took you round the country most of the time?

Carolyn Jay from Christian Aid was our facilitator. She speaks Arabic very well and she was the person who set up the itinerary and organised visits to particular places where Christian Aid partners would then show us around the area.

Did you go to any refugee camps?

Yes. We went to Daheisha refugee camp near Bethlehem and our guide there was from the Alternative Tourism Group. It was good to have a Palestinian guide for that. It was vital for us that we had a Jewish guide for some of the sites in West Jerusalem and Palestinian guides for most of the rest.

Did the visit modify or in any way affect your views on the political situation?

I knew some of the history. Before I was ordained I taught a GCSE course on the 'Arab-Israeli Conflict.' So I had the dates in my head—and the wars. And I had the Holocaust as the testing paradigm for the whole situation. I think that that changed while I was there and I came back much more aware of the current inequality and the current injustice which I think I hadn't been aware of before. I knew the history—bearing a time line in my mind—but it hadn't occurred to me what the current living situation was for Palestinians in Gaza and the West Bank. And having seen that, and experienced it, and had the hospitality of Palestinian families particularly— that was a very helpful corrective to my understanding, which had previously only been based on a Jewish narrative.

Has it strengthened the Liberation Theology dimension to your preaching?
I think it has. It has also strengthened the way I might describe the media in preaching as well. I do often mention the media in my preaching because I think that it is very potent force in society today. I am often rather critical of the media's role. But I have become more critical since I went to the Middle East because it became apparent to me quite soon that the information we were getting here was based upon a different agenda—all about balance. When something on the Palestinian side is mentioned this is immediately followed by something on the Israeli side but in fact it was all weighted towards the Israeli perspective.

In the current conflict I try to separate out in my mind criticisms of what is current Israeli policy—which is all I'm criticising—current and recent policy—rather than widening the criticisms to embrace wider issues.

You are not thinking about 1948 then?
I am looking more at the present. Of course, I understand that 1948 was either a triumph or a catastrophe. When I have heard Israelis—liberal Israelis— speaking, they have understood that too—that the State of Israel was bought at a huge cost to the Palestinians. I do understand that, but right now I would favour the two-state solution on the 1967 borders, that seems to me to be where we are now, practically speaking.

Some other questions … You obviously met the different Christian groups in the Holy Land did this experience in any way strengthen your ecumenical vision?
What I like about the group was that it was a Methodist and Anglican mix. I am quite strongly ecumenical and I was encouraged that we met different kinds of Christians active in *Sabeel*. It also encouraged me re-remembering that dialogue between faiths is really vital.

I was going to ask you about the interfaith dimension—whether your thinking and preaching had been affected in that area also.

Yes. I am impressed that the Palestinian people contain within them a magnificent inter-faith story in as much as they ask each other where are you from, rather than what religion they are. So the Muslim majority and the Christian minority, by and large get on fine. I suppose the historical feature of Jerusalem that really saddened me though—at the Church of the Holy Sepulchre was the way different Christian churches had their own places— that really made me very angry. I am probably being unfair here, but I thought, 'All men!'

Historically, of course, it was a policy of divide and rule by the Muslim rulers that contributed to that situation.

Yes, of course. I accept that. But in today's world—what is happening now? And women are marginal to that world—particularly in the Orthodox Church where women are not allowed into the sanctuary.

It is a different culture there, though. I told an Arab Orthodox friend of mine in Jordan about the ordination of women in the Church of England and he would not accept that I was not joking. He thought I was 'having him on.' How did you find that people reacted to female clergy? What reception did you as women clergy get from Palestinian Christians?

Absolutely fine! And we wore our clerical collars all the time as we were going around. So we were very visibly ordained. At the checkpoints we found that it actually helped.

We had one very funny evening with a group of women rabbis. Our Israeli guide was very funny. He was the only man there with a group of Christian women priests and Jewish women rabbis and he said, 'I am not going to say a thing all evening!' And we had a hilarious evening talking about what it was like to be public religious women in our different religious worlds.

Do you think that there might be a danger of mentioning the Holy Land too much in your preaching? Do you think that here is a danger of talking about the political issues too much? People might think, 'O, here she goes again!' Most ordinary people, after all, haven't a clue.

Yes. Particularly if you are in a parish and you are preaching week in, week out; there is a job of education to be done there, that you can do without constantly referring to the conflict. It's a question of language it's a question of naming occupation. You can even do it just by saying, 'Jesus lived under military occupation just as people do today under Israeli occupation in the Gaza Strip and the West Bank.' You can continue the process of education *without* constantly referring to, 'When I was in Palestine.' That really can just switch people off. I have preached twice specifically about the Holy Land since I came back, and once a whole sermon. And I got some very angry letters afterwards— particularly from Americans in the congregation. I went back and read the sermon and I think it really was balanced. I could argue that. But they were very angry to hear a Palestinian perspective.

It is interesting that they were Americans. I think that perhaps their media is even more partial than ours.

Yes, very much so. But they thought that it was an abuse of the pulpit to be talking about the issue at all. I was interested in that reaction and in a sense it politicised me going there and seeing the situation. But I am very definite that any criticisms that I want to make are about the policies of a democratic Israeli government in the occupied territories. I do not want to be open to the charge of anti-semitism because that is such a deeply rooted thing in the history of Christian thought—for example the prayers for Jews and infidels in the 1662 Prayer Book prayers on Good Friday—all that kind of nonsense. I am not going to buy into that. As I soon as I see it going in that direction I want to back off. For me it is a much wider issue about human rights. It is about the dignity of all people, whatever their ethnicity or religion. And as a Christian I am not neutral. I can't speak neutrally about it. I am already politicised—by being a Christian, by being British –but now I can speak with more knowledge.

Preaching responses

The concept of 'partners in preaching' inspired by Reuel L Howe,[4] proposes a faith sharing opportunity for members of the congregation that uses this approach. It is a device that can at once enable the preacher to obtain feedback from his or her preaching. It can also provide an opportunity for the hearer to articulate a response to the Word of God and thus for the church to be strengthened by the sharing of faith by its members. This approach converges with the understanding that all the baptised share in the priesthood of Christ and that all are called to hear the Gospel, live it out in

---

[4] R L Howe, *Partners in Preaching: Clergy and Laity in Dialogue*, The Seabury Press, New York, 1967. The summary of the standard procedure for groups using this method is based on a work sheet provided by Aquinas Institute of Theology, St Louis, Missouri.

their lives, and share in its proclamation. In this way it is hoped that the preacher will be affirmed and encouraged to continue the discipline of effective preaching.

The group gathers after the service. Usually it is not recommended that the preacher should be present for the discussion, which is audio-recorded. A facilitator chairs the discussion and ensures that every member of the group has an equal opportunity to contribute their ideas, that no one individual dominates, and that the discussion also not go beyond thirty minutes. For each of the four focus group reports described here, I decided to act as facilitator myself. The standard three questions asked by a facilitator are as follows: 1. How did God's Word and the homily touch your life today? 2. What difference will God's Word and the homily make in your week? 3. Are the ways in which today's preacher might have improved in communicating the message?

I also altered the phrasing of the questions in a way more appropriate to British culture and which I thought might expand the discussion beyond individualistic piety. Other questions specifically addressed Holy Land issues. In the cases of the Epiphany homily an additional question brought in the question of inter-faith understanding, and for the homily on the Samaritan Woman a question also was included on Christian ecumenism. These questions[5] also formed the basis of the focus group discussion based on the Iowa 'virtual pilgrimage.'

---

[5] 1.   In one sentence, say what (if anything) moved you in the preaching.

2.   What new insight (if any) did you gain from the preaching?

3.   In light of the preaching, how do you see the challenge of the text-to the individual?-to the Church?-to secular society?

4.   (Epiphany Homily) Please comment on how this preaching helped you to develop a greater sympathy and tolerance towards Judaism, Islam, and other world religions.

5.   (Samaritan Woman Homily) Please comment on how this preaching helped you to develop a greater sympathy and tolerance towards Christians of other traditions.

6.   (Epiphany Homily) As a result of this preaching, what new insights or awareness do you have about the beliefs and values shared by Christianity with Judaism and Islam?

7.   (Samaritan Woman Homily) As a result of this preaching, what new insights or awareness do you have about Christian unity?

8.   How did this preaching influence your understanding and attitude towards the Israeli-Palestinian conflict?

9.   In what way did this preaching elicit from you an active concern for the survival of the indigenous Christian communities in Israel-Palestine?

10.   How did this preaching help you to relate the political situation in Israel-Palestine to other situations of oppression and conflict at home and abroad?

11.   Please state briefly, in one sentence, what you heard as the central message of the preaching.

12.   In what way (if any) do you think the preaching could have been improved?

Epiphany homily at Clacton on Sea

The Epiphany homily (pp. 75-79) was preached at the eleven o'clock solemn Sunday Mass for the Feast of the Epiphany at Our Lady of Light Catholic Church in Clacton on Sea, Essex. This church is very well attended and has a large and active congregation. Clacton is a seaside town with a large number of retired people, the majority of whom would be politically conservative. The congregation at Our Lady of Light however reflects a wide spread of ages, outlooks, and backgrounds. I am able to preach at this church and its two daughter churches approximately every six weeks.

The group was made up of some fourteen parish stalwarts selected by the parish priest at my request. The group included an approximately even number of men and women with ages ranging from forty to seventy years.

The first member of the group to speak said that she was moved by the authority of the text and the way in which the homily made it relevant to situations in the modern world. Another participant was particularly struck by the contemporary relevance of otherwise arcane information on the return of the Jews from captivity in Babylon.

Several members of the group were affected by the articulation in the homily of the universal salvific will of God. They had already generally believed that sincere individuals of other religions and none would be able to find salvation but had not realised that this belief coincided with official Church teaching. Several added that they were previously unaware of the inclusivist teaching of Vatican II on non-Christian world religions and on the primacy of conscience. Other insights included the failure of the mass media to report world events faithfully and their corresponding concentration on trivia.

It was claimed that the preaching had not directly affected their attitude to other religions because they already had open and positive attitudes to other religions. However, one member of the group complained that Jews were 'insufficiently Christian,' and another thought that the positive references to Islam were too politically partisan in the light of the current debate over the inclusion of Turkey into an enlarged European Community. Another contributor warned of the danger of indifferentism and objected to my references to 'finding Christ' as too general since they did not specify the importance of belonging to the Catholic Church. Yet another contributor considered that I had emphasised Judaism at the expense of Islam while finding my positive statements about Judaism curiously at odds with the implied criticism of Israel in the references to the current political situation in the Holy Land.

On the issue of the Israeli-Arab dispute, none of the group expressed surprise or alarm at the perspective offered in the homily but added that it had generally confirmed their existing information and opinions.

Some found the homily thought provoking and challenging although others considered that the core message of the homily that Christ is the light at the centre of our experience was obscured by a rhetorical over-emphasis upon the power of darkness. While this may have been related to a desire for an unchallenging and reassuringly anodyne Gospel, this last criticism seemed, on reflection, to have some validity.

The Garasene Demoniac homily in Venice, Florida

This homily, on the Garasene Swine (pp. 46-48), was preached at a weekday Mass during an optional seminar for Aquinas Institute of Theology Doctor of Ministry in Preaching students in Venice, Florida. The group consisted of the celebrant, a Dominican professor of Homiletics, a deacon from Arizona, a female lay minister serving a Disciples of Christ congregation, a female religious on retreat at the centre, and my wife, a retired teacher of religious education.

All of the participants claimed that the preaching powerfully brought home a sense of the power and all pervasiveness of evil in the world. The antiphonal use of 'My name is Legion, there are hundreds of us!' had helped to produce this effect. The use of geography was noted, and the homily had been easy to follow.

On the issue of how the preaching had influenced the group's understanding and attitude towards the Israeli-Palestinian conflict, it was suggested that it had been clarified by the references to the experiences of the preacher. However, anxiety was expressed as to whether the preacher's blurring of the issue of the existence of evil spirits might lead to a failure both to address issues of systemic evil and to identify the moral responsibility of individuals. One participant asked whether I was letting Palestinian suicide bombers off the hook. The Israelis, it was claimed, were 'deeply wounded,' and it was suggested that it advisable to avoid taking sides. Another member of the group expressed appreciation that the devils were not only related to political evils but other more personal issues also.

Asked to state what was heard to be the central message suggestions were as follows: 'Evil drives people to madness and the power of evil is legion;' 'Jesus conquers evil and so should we;' 'Evil plays itself out in a multitude of ways and so does God' and 'Evil may seem to prevail but our hope is to overcome it.'

Several of the criticisms focussed on the ending, which was seen to be too abrupt ('jumping off the cliff with the pigs'). The opening by contrast was seen as strong, although the geographical detail was difficult to visualise. The transition to the Good News was not smooth enough, and the application was not adequately developed. The lack of balance between the detailed development of the problematic first move and the lack of detail in the Good News and its application was noted as weakness in the delivery. Meanwhile, divergent opinions about theological questions, concerning whether or how to demythologise the demonic and political questions about the legitimacy of taking a firm stand in favour of the Palestinians, remained unresolved.

The Samaritan Woman at the Well: a theme for Christian unity

The homily on John 4 (pp. 62–67) was given at the United Reformed Church in Twickenham as part of the celebration of the week of Prayer for Christian Unity. I have a happy ecumenical friendship with this small but committed congregation, and I am invited to preach at their main morning service four or five times a year. The number in the congregation seldom exceeds fifty, but there are no 'passengers' in the community. Every individual has an assigned ministry, and it is evident that the congregation has an above average level of theological knowledge and that they share a radical commitment on a range of social and political questions at home and overseas.

Twelve members of the congregation volunteered to stay behind to discuss the questions over coffee after the morning service. Responding to the question of what had moved them in the preaching, individuals gave a number of different answers. The fact of diversity among believers, whether Jews and Samaritans or Catholics and Protestants, was seen by one participant to be depressing: 'Nothing much has changed in two thousand years!' Another found the linking of the theme of Christian Unity with the story of the Samaritan Woman to have been both striking and helpful. Others were moved primarily by the preacher's account of the oppression of the Palestinians, which produced various responses ranging from anger over collective punishments to a general sense of despair and helplessness over the ongoing situation.

Asked about new insights, several people said that they found the historical background about the Samaritans to have been both useful and relevant. At the ecumenical level, the parallels between the disunity of Jews and Samaritans and the disunity of Christians today were seen as illuminating.

One respondent suggested that differences in both cases were secondary and man-made.

On the issue of how the preaching had influenced understandings and attitudes towards the Israeli-Palestinian conflict, it was suggested that it had made them more aware of the perceived American and Israeli bias in the British media. However, the entire group was already pro-Palestinian in outlook, and I was given the credit for having educated them on the matter on previous visits. Active concern for the survival of the indigenous Christian communities in the Holy Land was expressed by their commitment to the work of Christian Aid. Christian Aid is the development arm of Churches together in Great Britain and Ireland and is engaged in practical support for Palestinian projects, as well as in strong advocacy of Palestinian rights.

Members of the group claimed that the preaching had indeed helped them to make links in their minds between the political situation in Israel-Palestine and other situations of oppression. One respondent suggested that this linkage should move us to greater prayer, and another emphasised the necessity of Christian commitment to non-violence and to the advocacy of forgiveness over reprisal.

The central message of the preaching was summarised under the headings of challenge to break down barriers, the power of Jesus to change people and situations, hope for change, the necessity for reconciliation, the power of new beginnings through the power of love, and the shared need for 'Living Water.' No suggestions for improving the preaching were offered.

Good news for the poor

The United Reformed Church in Twickenham was again the locus of the last homily to be evaluated (pp. 100-05), the Preaching of Jesus at Nazareth (Luke 4: 18-30). This took place only three weeks after the previous visit to this congregation. The United Reformed Church is flexible in relation to set readings, and I was given the hospitality of the community so that I could preach on this text without waiting for it to appear in the Common Lectionary. The service included the following portions of Scripture: psalm 126 (recited antiphonally); Isaiah 61: 1-6; a sung paraphrase of the *Magnificat* and the Gospel reading. This was followed by the sermon and a taped discussion with congregation as 'Partners in Preaching' focus group.

The evening service was attended by eighteen persons, so it was easy to move forward and to invite the congregants to form 'buzz-groups' of two persons to exchange immediate thoughts and impressions before moving into a circle in front of the Communion Table for the discussion immediately after the homily. This has the advantage of giving members of the group the opportunity to register first thoughts so that discussion would flow more freely with nobody coming cold into the plenary discussion.

When asked what (if anything) moved them in the preaching, members of the group spoke of concern for the problem in the Holy Land and of gaining fresh motivation to do something about it. Personal recollections of the Holy Land by the preacher and the imaginative device pretending that they were in Nazareth on a pilgrimage were found to be helpful. One participant expressed appreciation for the way in which they had been asked to sympathise with the plight of the Jews before being led to greater concern for the Palestinians.

Several members of the group welcomed fresh insights derived from hitherto unfamiliar information about sources and dates of the three main sections of Isaiah, as this enabled them to see the text from Isaiah in historical context. Another spoke of the new insight from the preaching into the humanity of Jesus.

In light of the preaching, the text was seen as a challenge to the individual to act and to pray in the light of clearer information concerning the Israeli-Palestinian conflict. As a concrete expression of its renewed concern for the survival of the indigenous Christian communities in Palestine-Israel, the congregation agreed to donate funds towards a Living Stones scholarship at Bethlehem University to train Palestinian pilgrim guides. They also intended to march on the following Saturday on a demonstration against war on Iraq and for Palestinian rights. Another respondent resolved to devote more time to the study of the political issues.

On the question of how this preaching helped the hearers to relate the political situation in Israel-Palestine to other situations of oppression and conflict, it was suggested that the illustrations used had contributed effectively to that end. Another remarked that it was the responsibility of the listeners to make the connections recommended in the preaching. No improvements in the preaching were suggested.

Brief summaries of the content of the central message of the preaching included the following: 'Freedom for captives;' 'Promise of Sion;' 'We must translate words into actions' and 'The freeing of prisoners is up to me.'

Virtual pilgrimage

The 'virtual pilgrimage' was preached in December 2002 at the Catholic Chaplaincy at Iowa State University. Both schemas, set out in outline here, were employed for two separate 'retreat groups,' the first lasting four hours and the second three. All but two of the homiletic presentations preached at the 'stations' on the journey were based upon texts from Luke, which were used in both schemas.

The first schema was based upon an experience-based pilgrimage itinerary, offering a realistic tour schedule, and the second shorter schema was based upon the travels of Jesus as presented in the Gospel of Luke. At each stage of the imaginary journey there was a mixture of Bible readings, historical and topical commentary, and spiritual reflections interspersed with short intervals for quiet meditation. At several points in the imaginary itinerary there were formal homilies based upon preaching plans set out in the earlier sections of this work.[6] The presentation of both schemas involved the use of an amateur video made during a student pilgrimage that I had led in 1999, supplemented by a professionally produced video. Clips were played from both of these video-recordings and maps were used, with pauses for input of background geographical, biblical, historical and contemporary information. Still photographs with the use of an overhead projector illustrated each of the 'stations' for brief homiletic presentation and silent reflection.

The cognitive and affective aims of both itineraries were as follows.

Cognitive Aims
—To provide geographical background to the Gospel narratives and the history of Christian pilgrimage to the Holy Land
—To give basic physical geographical information about Jerusalem and the Holy Land together with some basic historical information about the State of Israel and the city of Jerusalem
—To familiarise the 'pilgrims' with the monuments and shrines of the Holy Land
—To familiarise the group with the ecumenical and pluralistic character of the Holy Land and to enhance historical and

---

[6] Summaries of both itineraries are included on pages 174–8 of Duncan Macpherson, 'Preaching and the Holy Land', 2003. The thesis is available at the library of the Aquinas Institute and as a link at the website on www.deaconduncan.com.

ecumenical understanding of the variety of Jewish, Muslim, and Christian presence in the Holy Land

—To provide historical perspectives and insights into the modern political conflict between Israelis and Palestinians

Affective Aims

—To communicate sense of the excitement of a pilgrim group arriving at the gates of Jerusalem for the first time

—To communicate a sense of the importance of Jerusalem to the believers of the three religions of Christianity, Islam, and Judaism

—To share the 'wilderness experience' experienced by John the Baptist and by Jesus at the time of his temptation in the desert

—To stimulate the imagination to share in the events of Holy Week and to make connections between the sufferings of Christ and those of refugees and others caught up in situations of exile and oppression

—To strengthen faith in the resurrection of Christ and to foster an active concern for the survival of indigenous Christian communities

—To provide a framework for deepening faith in the Incarnation and becoming committed to the liberation of the oppressed

—To provide the opportunity to explore links between Christian faith and the struggles with evil in the Holy Land and elsewhere in the world

Feedback from Iowa

The focus group evaluating the virtual pilgrimage included the Catholic Chaplain of the University who also functioned as the moderator. Among the other members of the focus group was a young college female who is interested in a career in ministry and dedicated to social justice and wanting to do follow up on the Palestinian issue. Another was a biblically educated woman religious in her fifties who has never been to the Holy Land. Both these two were members of the Chaplaincy team. Others included a female parish liturgist in her fifties, a young male undergraduate, a 46 years old male engineer, highly educated and a dedicated member of the chaplaincy's own regular partners in the preaching group.

In answer to the question of what (if anything) moved the hearers in the preaching of the 'virtual pilgrimage', direct quotations included the following.

'We thank Duncan for being here and sharing with us so much information,' and, 'He surely stretched our awareness of the places where Jesus walked.' One member of the focus group wrote to me as follows: 'Thank you for your presentation on Sunday. You have a wealth of information to share, and you share it articulately. I only wish that we would all feel secure enough about visiting the area to enlist you as a pilgrimage leader. You certainly whetted our appetites for such a trip. We are so sorry that we haven't made the trip before now. It would be such a privilege to walk in the pathway of Jesus accompanied by the scripture readings and the historical perspectives which you know so well.'

Others were moved by the predicament of the people of the land, as well as by images of the places: 'I was moved by the sights of the people and places so embedded in our minds historically ... and how they look today ... still very much in keeping with what our mind pictures. It was surely communicated how the people of that region have undergone so much in history and yet generations later still surviving ... many in difficult circumstances.'

On new insights gained from the preaching, at the historical level the group welcomed the remedying of perceived ignorance of the historical background to the topics and issues treated in the presentation. According to one member of the group, the presentation was 'very educational particularly for those of us who have not had a chance to travel there and whose information primarily comes from the press ... It was very worthwhile to work on this and to offer it to others.' The group registered the comments of many of those who had attended that had expressed their gratitude at 'the learning they accomplished by attending the various talks/lecture.'

Commenting on the influence on their understanding and attitude towards the Israeli-Palestinian conflict, the group seemed to concur with the comment, 'Those that were aware of the depth of suffering were glad to have an advocate for the Palestinian people. The explanation of the peoples and the divisions of territory clarified for me the background and the understanding of the many conflicts. The future of so many people will probably always be coloured by conflicts or the past knowledge of those conflicts.'

Asked in what way did the preaching had elicited active concern, there was some concern about what to do for follow up, 'so that this doesn't remain an activity that's left on the intellectual level, but leads to action inspired by faith.'

Those who attended both sessions had almost all found the second schema, based on Luke's Gospel, more personally rewarding. One member of the focus group who had attended only the first session regretted that that there had not been more of a 'spiritual emphasis.' By this she meant 'prayer, scripture, and sharing instead of a travelogue', but added, 'When you did use scripture it was meaningful.'

Outstanding issues and questions

The limitations in size and range of the research samples included in my research did not permit of any decisive conclusions. Rather, they provided impressions of ideas and responses from a range of groups and individuals and may be seen as offering hypotheses that could be tested more scientifically in some other study.

Issues and questions highlighted by responses in each of these empirical venues can be broadly divided into the categories of the political and the theological.

Among the political issues and questions there was an acknowledged ignorance of the politics of the Israeli–Palestinian dispute. A recurrent example of this was evident in comments suggesting that the conflict was 'thousands of years old'. The British media were consistently blamed for distorted or pro-Israeli bias but were seen to compare well with the American media. This might account for the difference between the more pro-Palestinian responses of British respondents on the one hand and the outright anger of the American tourists writing to Lucy Winkett or the more guardedly neutral responses of the Fisher's Net respondents on the other. The majority of those who were moved by accounts of Palestinian sufferings raised the question of how their concern could be expressed at the practical level. The interview with Lucy Winkett also raised the issue of whether it was possible—or desirable—to keep criticism of present Israeli policies separate from an examination of the morality of the setting up of the State of Israel in 1948.

Among the most important of the primarily theological issues raised by the research was a general absence of an adequate hermeneutic either for preaching or for interpreting Holy Land issues. Responses suggested a lack of awareness of any wider Liberation Theology perspective within which to place the Palestinian issue. Another hermeneutical lacuna related to the problem of the interpretation of Old Testament readings in ways that might condone injustice.

Importantly in the present international climate, Christian–Muslim relations did not seem to figure as an issue for many. Moreover, although Jewish–Christian relations seemed to be an issue for some respondents, knowledge or concern for inter-faith relations seemed generally to be underdeveloped, the more so among American respondents. Experience suggests that where the issue of inter-faith is raised in homilies congregations respond positively. In this respect, it was interesting that the Catholic focus group at Our Lady of Light Church were ignorant of the positive official Church teachings in this area. Finally, a number of people raised questions about the problematic relationship between Jewish–Christian dialogue and critiques either of Zionism or of Israeli policies.

CONCLUSION

This study has been a multidisciplinary survey of the relationship between the Holy Land and preaching and has argued throughout that the Holy Land has a relevance for preaching that is not limited to those who preach to groups of pilgrims visiting the land. Indeed, it has proposed that the Holy Land has a more general application to preaching everywhere. It has agued, too, for a relevance that goes well beyond a useful understanding of the geography of first century Palestine. Instead, it has proposed the importance to preaching of the land in all its aspects and in all the periods of its history up to and including today.

It is evident that understanding of the Holy Land, like the message it informs, is always mediated and refracted through the insights, prejudices, and experience both of the preacher and of the hearers of the message. This has been validated against the historical perspective of the relationship between preaching and pilgrimage to the Holy Land over the centuries. Modern critical theory has provided us with some useful tools for exploring the relevance of the world of the Holy Land for understanding and applying the preaching of the Christian message. In the context of this discourse the Holy Land is not only indispensable for our knowledge of 'the world behind the text,' but it is also part of 'the world in front of the text' that provides the hermeneutical framework for Christian theology and homiletics.

I have argued, too, that the historical and contemporary religious diversity of the Holy Land provides an inspiration and a paradigm for both ecumenical and multi-faith preaching as well as an active concern for the welfare and the survival of the indigenous Christian communities.

Perhaps more controversially, I have pressed the case that the realities of the contemporary Israeli-Palestinian conflict provide a context for exploring a Liberation Theology hermeneutic in preaching. During the period in which this study was written, news from the Holy Land has become progressively worse. Sadly, there seems to be no prospect for a resolution of the conflict in the foreseeable future. This links in with what Mary Catherine Hilkert characterises as the preaching of 'grace at the edges' within 'the contemporary experience of impasse.' Here 'the preacher 'names grace' but, especially in the contrast experiences of life, it is equally important that the preacher names the situations of impasse and 'dis-grace,' or sin, that confront creation and call out for redemption.'[1]

The final chapter inquired into the experiences of preachers who have been pilgrims to the Holy Land and examined the responses of partners in preaching groups to some of my own homilies. This research bears out the general thesis offered here, but it also suggests that much work needs to be done before the Israeli-Palestinian impasse can be integrated into a more general understanding of how Christian preaching can begin to challenge structures and situations of oppression and injustice everywhere.

---

[1] Hilkert, *op. cit.*, 111.

BIBLIOGRAPHY

Abdelaziz A Ayyad, *Arab Nationalism and the Palestinians,* PASSIA, Jerusalem, 1999.

Anawati, G, 'The Roman Catholic Church and the Churches in Communion with Rome', A J Arberry, (ed.) *Religion in the Middle East,Volume 1: Judaism and Christianity*, University Press Cambridge: Cambridge, 1969, 347-422.

Anon., *Calendars of Entries in the Papal Registers relating to Great Britain and Ireland. 3, 605.* Cited in Webb, *op. cit.*, 287.

Anon., *New York Times*, 26 November 1964.

Anon., *Herder Correspondence*, March 1965.

Anon, *Documents on Jerusalem*, PASSIA (Palestinian Academy Society for the Study of International Affairs), Jerusalem, 1996.

Armstrong, K, *A History of Jerusalem: One City Three Faiths*, HarperCollins, London, 1996.

Anon, *The Guardian*, London, 23 October 2002.

Anon, *The World Guide. An Alternative Guide to the Countries of our Planet 2001/ 2002*, New Internationalist Publications, Oxford, 2001, 302.

Bentwich N, in A J Arberry, *Religion in the Middle East,Volume 1: Judaism and Christianity*, University Press Cambridge: Cambridge, 1969, 59-118.

Blenkinsopp, Joseph, 'Second Isaiah-Prophet of Universalism', P Davies ed., *The Prophets,* Sheffield Academic Press, Sheffield, England, 1996, 97ff.

Boff, C, 'Epistemology and Methodology of the Theology of Liberation', Ellacuria, Ignacio and Jon Sobrino, eds., *Mysterium Liberationis. Fundamental Concepts of Liberation Theology,* Orbis, Maryknoll, New York, 1993, 57-85

Buttrick, D, *Homiletic: Moves and Structures, Part I*, Fortress Press, Philadelphia, 1987.

Chadwick, Henry, *The Circle and the Ellipse: Rival Concepts of Authority in the Early Church*, Inaugural Lecture, Oxford University Press, 1959.

Cohn-Sherbok, Lavinia, 'Judaism', John Bowker, ed., *The Oxford Dictionary of World Religions,* Oxford University Press, Oxford 1997, 270-1.

Collins, Raymond F, *Introduction to the New Testament*, SCM Press, London, 1983.

Council of Churches for Britain and Ireland, *A New Way of Thinking. Guidelines for the Churches*, Council of Churches for Britain and Ireland, Commission for Inter-Faith Relations: Christians and Jews, Council of Churches for Britain and Ireland, London, 1994.

Council for the Advancement of Arab British Understanding, London (Intifada Facts Sheet, February 2003) and B'tselem (Israeli Information Center for Human Rights) http: //www.btselem.org.

Craddock, Fred, *As One Without Authority,* Chalice Press, St Louis, Mo.

Cragg, Kenneth, 'The Anglican Church' , A J Arberry, ed., *Religion in the Middle East*, vol. 1, Cambridge University Press, Cambridge, 1969, 570-595.

Cragg, Kenneth, *Palestine. The Prize and Price of Zion,* Cassell, London and Washington, 1997.

Davis, Uri, *Israel, An Apartheid State,* Zed Books, London and New Jersey, 1987.

Dornisch, Loretta C, *A Woman Reads Luke,* Collegeville, Liturgical Press, Minnesota, 1999.

Drinan, Robert F, *Honor the Promise,* Doubleday, Cape Town and New York, 1977.

Edwards, Beverly M, *Islamic Politics in Palestine,* Tauris, London, 1996.

Eliade Mercea, *Sacred and Profane*, trans. W R Trask, Harcourt Bruce and World, Inc., New York, 1959.

Evans, Craig A, 'Third Sunday after Epiphany, Year C', in Roger E van Harn, ed., *The Lectionary Commentary, Theological Exegesis of Sunday's Texts, The Third readings: the Gospels,* Eerdmans, Grand Rapids, Michigan, 2001, 325-8.

Flannery, Austin, OP, ed., *Vatican II: Constitutions; Decrees; Translations, A Completely Revised translation in Inclusive Language*, Costello Publications New York and Dominican Publications, Dublin, 1982.

Flannery, Edward H, and Eugene Fisher, 'Israel, Jerusalem, and the Middle East', A James Rudin and Marc Tannenbaum, eds., *Twenty Years of Jewish-Catholic Relations*, Paulist, Maywah, New York, 1986, 73-86.

Fleer, David, 'Shaped by Story', 'The Promise and Premise of Autobiography for Preaching', David Fleer and Dave Bland, eds., *Preaching Autobiography: Connecting the World of the Preacher to the World of the Text, Rochester College Lectures on Preaching,* Vol. 2., ACU Press, Abilene, Texas, 2001, 23-46.

Gee, John, *Unequal Conflict, The Palestinians and the Israelis*, Pluto Press, London, 1998.

Gibb, H A R, and J H Kramers 'Kubbat al Sakhra', cited in *Concise Encyclopaedia of Islam*, E J Brill, Leiden, 1974, 267-269.

Gilbert, Martin, *Israel, A History*, Doubleday, London and New York, 1998.

Gregory of Nyssa, *Life of Holy Macrina*, ed. Ducaeus/Gretser, *Patrologia Graeca 46*, trans. H O Ogle, *Nicene and Post Nicene Fathers*, Oxford University Press, Oxford, 1890-1900.

Hall, Douglas John, *Thinking the Faith: Christian Theology in a North American Context*, Fortress Press, Minneapolis, 1991.

Hall, Douglas, *Professing the Faith: Christian Theology in a North American Context*, Fortress Press, Minneapolis, 1996.

Halperin, Samuel, *The Political World of American Zionism*, Wayne State University Press, Detroit, Michigan , 1961.

Hanson, K C, and D E Oakman, *Palestine in the Time of Jesus-Social Structures and Social Conflicts*, Augsburg Press, Minneapolis 1998.

Harrelson, Walter, and Randall M Falk, *Jews and Christians: A Troubled Family*, Abingdon, Nashville, 1990.

Harrington, D, *Sacra Pagina: The Gospel of Matthew*, ed. Daniel J Harrington, Liturgical Press, Collegeville, Minnesota 1991.

Heacock, Roger, 'International Politics and Sectarian Policy in the Late Ottoman Period', Thomas Hummel et al., eds., *Patterns of the Past, Prospects for the Future: The Christian Heritage in the Holy Land*, Melisende, London, 1999.

Hegstad, Harald, 'Der Erloeser der Heiden oder Israels Messias? Zur Frage der theologischen und christologischen Bedeutung des Judeseins Jesu,' *Kerygma und Dogma*, 40, 1994, 33-44. English 'Saviour of the Gentiles or Israel's Messiah?' trans. B A Asen, *Theology Digest*, Summer 1997, 111-116.

Herzl, T, *The Jewish State*, Dover Editions, New York, 1988.

Herzl, T, *The Complete Diaries Of Theodor Herzl*, vol. 1, ed., Raphael Patain, trans. Harry Zohn, Herzl Press, New York, 1960.

Hilliard, Alison, and Betty J Bailey, *Living Stones Pilgrimage*, Cassell, London, 1999.

Hilkert, Mary Catherine, *Naming Grace Preaching and the Sacramental Imagination*, Continuum, New York, 1997.

Horner, Norman, *A Guide to the Christian Churches in the Middle East*, Elkhart, Mission Focus, Indiana, 1989.

Hornus, Jean Michel, 'The Lutheran and Reformed Churches', A J Arberry, ed., *Religion in the Middle East, Volume 1: Judaism and Christianity*, Cambridge University Press, Cambridge, 1969.541, 534-569.

Hooker, M, *The Gospel of Mark*, A and C Black, London, 1991.

Housley, N, *The Crusaders*, Tempus, London, 2002.

Hummel, Ruth, and Thomas Hummel, *Patterns of the Sacred. English Protestant and Russian Orthodox Pilgrims of the Nineteenth Century*, Scorpion Cavendish, London, 1995

Hunt, E D, *Holy Land Pilgrimage in the Later Roman Empire AD 312-460*, Clarendon Press, Oxford, 1984.

Hughes, O O, *The Reading and Preaching of the scriptures in the Worship of the Christian Church*, Volume 2, The Patristic Age, Eerdmans, Grand Rapids, Michigan, 1998.

Jacobs, Daniel, *Israel and the Palestinian Territories, Rough Guide*, Rough Guides, London, 1998.

Jacobs, Louis, *The Jewish Religion, A Companion*, Oxford University Press, Oxford, 1995.

John, R, and S Hadawi, *The Palestine Diary*, vol. I, 1914-1945, the Palestine Research Centre, Beirut, Lebanon, 1970.

Johnson, Luke Timothy, *The Gospel of Luke, Sacra Pagina*, ed. Daniel J Harrington, The Liturgical Press Collegeville, Minnesota, 1991.

Karris, Robert J, 'The Gospel According to Luke', R E Brown, *et al.*, eds., *The New Jerome Biblical Commentary*, Geoffrey Chapman, London, 1990, 675-721.

Khalidi, Walid, *Palestine Reborn,* Tauris, London and New York, 1992.

Khalidi, Walid, ed., *All That Remains, The Palestinian Villages Occupied and Depopulated in Israel*, Institute for Palestine Studies, Washington DC, 1992.

Kselman, J, and R Witherup, 'Modern New Testament Criticism,' R Brown *et al.*, eds., *The New Jerome Biblical Commentary*, Geoffrey Chapman, London, 1990, 1130-1145

Küng, Hans, *Judaism*, trans. J Bowker, SCM, London, 1992.

Laqueur, Walter, ed., *The Israeli Arab Reader, A Documentary History of the Middle East Conflict*, Weidenfeld and Nicolson, London, 1969.

Lestschinsky, Jacob, 'Jewish Migrations, 1840-1956', Louis Finkelstein, *The Jews, Their History, Culture and Religion,* vol. 2, Peter Owen, London, 1961, 1536-1598.

Laurentin, René, and J Neusner, 'The Declaration on the relation of the Church to non-Christian Religions', *Commentary on the Documents of Vatican II*, Herder, New York, 1966.

Lowry, E, *The Homiletical Plot: The Sermon as Narrative Art Form*, Westminster John Knox Press, Atlanta, 1980.

Mango, Marla Maria, 'Pilgrimage', Cyril. Mango, ed., *The Oxford History of Byzantium,* Oxford University Press, Oxford, 2002.

Macpherson, Duncan, 'Letter from Bir Zeit', *Middle East International,* 26 March 1982.

Macpherson, Duncan, 'Letter from Bethlehem', *Middle East International,* 19 December 1987.

Macpherson, Duncan, 'Living Stones and Living Faith,' Michael Prior, ed., *They Came and They Saw,* London, Melisende, 2000, 57-68.

Macpherson, Duncan, ed., *A Third Millennium Guide to the Holy Land,* Melisende, London, 2000.

Malina, B, and R Rohrbraugh, *Social-Science Commentary on the Synoptic Gospels,* Fortress Press, Minneapolis, 1992.

Malina, B, and R Rohrbaugh, *Social Science Commentary on the Gospel of John,* Fortress Press, Minneapolis, 1998.

Mansfield, Peter, *Arab History of the Middle East,* Viking, London, 1991.

Masahla, Nur *A Land Without a People,* Pluto, London, 1997.

Menucci, Garay, 'Kulthum Auda, Palestinian Ethnographer: Gendering the Palestinian Landscape', in Abu Lughod *et al.* eds., *Landscape of Palestine: Equivocal Poetry,* West Bank Publications, Birzeit University, Birzeit, 1999, 79-96.

Moloney, F, *Sacra Pagina: The Gospel of John,* Daniel J Harrington, ed., Collegeville Liturgical Press, Minnesota 1998.

Morris, Benni, ed., *The Birth of the Palestinian Refugee Problem, 1947-49* Oxford University Press, Oxford, 1987.

Molinier A, and Ch. Kohler, *Descriptiones Terrae Sanctae ex saec.,* VIII, IX, XII, XV Geneva, 1885, and T Tobler, Leipzig, 1874. Cited in Prawer, *op. cit.,* 546.

Newman, John H, *Catena Aurea, Commentary on the Four Gospels Collected Out of the Works of the Fathers by Saint Thomas Aquinas, Volume Three: Saint Luke,* The Saint Austin Press, Southampton, 1997, (first published in English in 1941).

Nickle, Keith F, *Preaching the Gospel of Luke: Proclaiming God's Rule,* Westminster Knox, Louisville, Kentucky, 2000.

O'Connor, Jerome Murphy, *The Holy Land: An Archaeological Guide From the Earliest Times To 1700,* Oxford University Press, Oxford, 1986.

Old, Hugh Oliphant, *The Reading and Preaching of the Scriptures in the Worship of the Christian Church,* Volume 2, The Patristic Age, Eerdmans, Grand Rapids, Michigan, 1998.

Old, Hugh Oliphant, *The Preaching of the Scriptures in the Worship of the Christian Church,* Volume 3, *The Medieval Church,* Eerdmans, Grand Rapids and

Michigan and Cambridge, England, 1999.

O'Mahony, Anthony, 'The Religious, Political and Social Status of the Christian Communities in Palestine', in A O'Mahony, *et al.*, eds., *The Christian Heritage in the Holy Land,* Scorpion Cavendish, London, 1995, 237-265.

Pawlikowski, John, 'Ethical Issues in the Israeli Palestinian Conflict,' in R Reuther and M Ellis, eds., *Beyond Occupation: American Jews, Christians and Palestinians*: Beacon Press, Boston, 1990, 155-70.

Pazdan, Margaret, 'Third Sunday in Lent, Year A,' R van Harn, *The Lectionary Commentary: Theological Exegesis for Sunday's Texts. The Third Readings: The Gospels*, Eerdmans, Grand Rapids, 2001, 501-5.

Prawer, Joshua, *The Crusaders' Kingdom: European Colonialism in the Middle Ages*, Phoenix Press, London, 2001 (Hardback edition, Praeger, New York, 1972).

Prior, Michael, *Jesus the Liberator, Nazareth Liberation Theology (Luke 4. 16-30),* Sheffield Academic Press, Sheffield, England, 1995.

Prior, Michael, *The Bible and Colonialism*, Sheffield Academic Press, Sheffield, 1997.

Prior, Michael, *Zionism and the State of Israel, A Moral Inquiry*, Routledge, London, 1999.

Prior, Michael, 'Speaking Truth in the Jewish-Christian Dialogue', *A Faithful Presence*, in eds., Thomas David with Clare Amos, Melisende, London, 2003, 327-47.

Prior, Michael, and Nur Masalha, 'Introducing the Journal', *Holy Land Studies,* Vol. 1, Num. 1, Sheffield Academic Press, Sheffield, 2002, 5-7.

Regan, Geoffrey, *First Crusader: Byzantium's Holy Wars*, Sutton Publishing, Stroud, 2001.

Reed, Carson, 'The Promise and Premise of Autobiography for Preaching', David Fleer, and Dave Bland, eds., *Preaching Autobiography: Connecting the World of the Preacher to the World of the Text, Rochester College Lectures on Preaching*, Vol. 2., ACU Press, Abilene, Texas, 2001, 97-124.

Reiss, Moshe, 'Jewish Fundamentalism', *Holy Land Hollow Jubilee, God Justice and the Palestinians,* Naim Ateek and M. Prior, Melisende, eds., London, 1999, 168-179.

Renoux, Charles, *Hesychius of Jerusalem, Homilies sur Job.* (Armenian text with French translation), *Patrologies Orientalis*, vol. 42, Brepols, Turnhout, 1938.

Resner, Andre (Jr), *Preacher and Cross: Person and Message in Theology and Rhetoric*, Eerdmans, Grand Rapids, 1999.

Richards, Hubert, 'Thoughts on a Journey', *Scripture Bulletin*, Volume 5, number 2.

Winter 1974-5, Catholic Biblical Association of Great Britain, London, 33-5.

Rousseau, John, and Rami Arav, *Jesus and His World. An Archaeological and Cultural Dictionary*, Fortress Press, Minneapolis, 1995.

Rynne, Xavier, *The Fourth Session*, Faber and Faber, London, 1966.

Sabeel, http://www.sabeel.org/news/newslt15/matar.html

Sabella, Bernard, in 'Socio-Economic Characteristics and Challenges', in Michael Prior and William Taylor, eds., *Christians in the Holy Land,* World of Islam Festival Trust, London, 1994, 38-39.

Schölch, Alexander, 'Jerusalem in the Nineteenth Century,' K J Asali *et al.*, eds., *Jerusalem in History,* Scorpion, London, 1989, 228-248.

Said, Edward, 'Memory, Invention and Space' in I Abu Lughod, *et al*, eds., *Landscape of Palestine: Equivocal Poetry,* University Publications, Birzeit, West Bank, 1999, 3-22.

Schöleh, A, *Palestine in Transformation, 1856-1882, Studies in Social, Economic and Political Development*, Institute for Palestine Studies, Washington DC 1993.

Sharif, Regina, *Non-Jewish Zionism, Its Roots in Western History*, Zed Books, London, 1983.

Schneiders, Sandra M, *The Revelatory Text: Interpreting the New Testament as Sacred Scripture,* Liturgical Press, Collegeville, Minnesota, 1999.

Sobrino, John, *Jesus in Latin America,* Orbis, Maryknoll, New York, 1987.

Stanton, Graham N, 'The Communities of Matthew' in Kingsbury, Jack Dean eds., *Gospel Interpretation: Narrative Critical and Social Scientific Approaches,* Trinity Press, Harrisburg, Pennsylvania, 1997, 49-64.

Stevens, R P, *American Zionism and US Foreign Policy, 1942-7,* Institute for Palestine Studies, Pageant Press, New York, 1962.

Stuhlmueller, Carroll, 'Deutero-Isaiah and Trito-Isaiah', in Raymond Brown *et al.* (eds.), *The New Jerome Biblical Commentary,* Geoffrey Chapman, London, 1989, 329-348.

Sufimaster, http://www.sufimaster.org. web site at www.napanet.net.

Tanenbaum, M H, 'A Jewish Viewpoint on Nostra Aetate,' in E Fisher and A J Rudin, eds., *Twenty Years of Jewish Catholic Relations*, Paulist Press, Maywah, New York, 1986, 58-59.

Tessler, M, *A History of the Israeli-Palestinian Conflict*, Indiana University Press, Bloomington and Indianapolis, 1974.

Tisdale, Leonora, *Preaching as Local Theology and Folk Art*, Fortress Press, Minneapolis, 1997.

Tobler, T, and A Molinier, eds., *Itinera Hierosolymtiana et descriptiones Terrae Sanctae bellis sacris anteriora et latina lingua exarata,* I, 1-2 vols, Geneva, 1872. Cited in Prawer, *op. cit.*, 546.

Van Buren, Paul, *Discerning the Way: A Theology of Jewish Christian Reality,* Seabury, New York, 1980.

Walsh, Michael, *A Dictionary of Devotions,* Burns Oates, London, 1993.

Wagner, Donald, 'Reagan and Begin, Bibi and Jerry: The Theopolitical Alliance of the Likud Party with the American Christian Right', N Ateek and M Prior, eds., *Holy Land, Hollow Jubilee,* Melisende, London, 1998, 199-215.

Donald Wagner, 'Anxious for Armageddon; Probing Israel's Support among American Fundamentalists', H Haddad and D Wagner, eds., *All in the Name of the Bible,* Amana Books, Brattelboro, Vermont, 1986, 201-2.

Webb, Diane, *Pilgrimage in Medieval England,* Hambledon and London, London and New York, 2000.

Webb, J, *Preaching and the Challenge of Pluralism,* Chalice Press, St Louis Missouri, 1998, 99.

Wilson, Paul Scott, 'Third Sunday of Easter, Year A', E Harn, ed., *The Lectionary Commentary. The Third Readings: The Gospels,* Continuum, New York and London, 2001, 464-8.

Wilken, Robert, *The Land Called Holy. Palestine in Christian History and Thought,* Yale University Press, Newhaven and London, 1992.

Wilkinson, John, *Egeria's Travels, Newly translated with supporting documents,* Aris and Philips, Warminster, 1999.

Wilkinson, John, *Jerusalem Pilgrimages Before the Crusades,* Aris and Philips Warminster, 2002, England.

Zureik, E T, *The Palestinians in Israel; A Study in Inner Colonialism,* Routledge and Kegan Paul, London, 1979.

BIBLICAL REFERENCES

INDEX